The Barnsdale Handy Gardener

John Pilgrim – Nick and Sue Hamilton

Photography by David Thrower

Illustrations by Johanna Pilgrim

www.barnsdalegardens.co.uk
marketing@barnsdalegardens.co.uk

www.redshift-photography.co.uk
david.thrower@redshift-photography.co.uk

www.alpine-press.co.uk
sales@alpine-press.co.uk

www.outsidegardendesign.co.uk

In memory of dad, Jack Darlington

Sue Hamilton

ISBN 0-9528631-6-2

Contents

The Team

Nick Hamilton developed his passion for gardening when his father purchased a derelict garden centre in Kettering. He worked with his dad at weekends and during school holidays. He trained at Writtle College and took a National Diploma course in commercial horticulture before joining Darby Nursery Stock in Norfolk, one of the largest wholesale container nurseries in the country. After gaining valuable experience at other nurseries he purchased a piece of land in Rutland in 1989. This land formed the nursery and part of Barnsdale Gardens. Sue Hamilton was brought up on a farm so a move into horticulture was no great shock to her system. She started work at Barnsdale in 1983 when Geoff purchased the current site as a ploughed field. She was employed as gardener/secretary. Sue's natural talent for all things horticultural blossomed. Sue now designs the show gardens and displays exhibited by Barnsdale Gardens at all the major gardening shows. She has developed a talent for container planting at Barnsdale and hosts courses on the subject. John Pilgrim worked at Simmonds Nurseries in Hertfordshire in the early sixties. He moved on to work with his brother as a landscape gardener. In 1965 John moved to Suffolk where he ran his own horticultural contracting firm until he was lured into other things. After a varied working career, John settled into the life of broadcasting with the BBC and he also works as a freelance writer and journalist. David Thrower travels the world in search of the right picture. He began his career as a sports photographer and then spent several years in the lighting industry. David and his wife Melanie run their own highly successful photography business which has an extensive and varied client base.

Introduction

At the time of his death on August 4th 1996 Geoff Hamilton was arguably Britain's best known gardener. His regular appearances on BBC television's *'Gardeners' World'* were eagerly awaited each week by legions of fans. It is not hard to understand Geoff's popularity because he was quite simply the gardener's gardener who told it like it was and if Geoff Hamilton had a gimmick, it was his ability to communicate his love of all things horticultural to the millions who tuned in to watch him on television. You do not cultivate that type of gimmick, you are born with it. Barnsdale Gardens were Geoff's brainchild. He found the land, realised its potential and became a child again when it came to ploughing his five acres of England in preparation for what was to become a unique gardening experience. Geoff's son Nick will tell you that 'the old man' took no prisoners when it came to garden design and layout, he simply got on with encouraging people like me to get out there on my own modest plot and enjoy!

I met Nick and Sue Hamilton in 2003 while I was on a visit to Rutland where I visited a local pub. I don't recall the name because I spent a pleasant evening in the company of the landlord who insisted I should sample the contents of the 'top shelf' with him, but I do remember the landlord's parting words as I made my way back to where I thought I had parked my caravan. "You must visit Barnsdale Gardens," he bellowed. In fact as I recall it came out, "You mushed visist Barnshdale Gardens." The next morning I remembered my new friend's advice and happened upon a brand new cure for a hangover. From the moment I walked into the gardens my headache decreased and as I ambled through this haven of peace and tranquillity I was a gardener again! By the time I left I was already planning changes to my own modest plot and I had the advice of Nick and Sue ringing in my ears to spur me on.

It cannot be denied that Geoff Hamilton was a hard act to follow but

Nick and Sue have achieved success beyond 'the old man's' dreams. They could have gone down a purely commercial road and cashed in on Geoff's reputation but they didn't and instead they remained true to the Barnsdale tradition. It is true that you can see the gardens designed and constructed by Geoff Hamilton but you will see much more besides. Sue has designed several new gardens including a Japanese garden and Nick has constructed the Tea House for this garden and still managed to watch his beloved Tottenham Hotspur on the days Sue gave him off! They are as committed to organic gardening as Geoff ever was. Nick says, "Being a gardener is like being a Spurs supporter, you start each season in hope of something better!" Sue (who is not a Spurs supporter) says, "Being a Spurs supporter gives him plenty of time to spend in the garden because Spurs tend to spend very little time in the FA Cup or any other cup competitions!" I am fortunate to have become friends with two people who spend the best part of their lives gardening and sharing their knowledge with others. This is the first gardening book to come out of Barnsdale for ten years and I hope that you will enjoy learning about 'Proper gardening the Barnsdale Way'. It is for you, a real gardener.

John Pilgrim, Sandy,
Bedfordshire 2006.

Part One – Choice Plants

Nick and Sue have selected a variety of shrubs that you might want to consider growing in your garden. The list is not exhaustive and you will find other examples at your local plant or garden centre or indeed at Barnsdale, but before you select something do seek expert advice and do make sure that it *is* expert advice! There is nothing wrong with buying the odd plant or three from your local supermarket or indeed at a 'knock down price' from elsewhere but do remember, if you want some instant colour, the old adage, 'If it seems too good to be true it probably is'. Too often in the past I have been persuaded to buy a plant in full bloom simply because I wanted an instant impact in my garden and this is understandable, provided that you have money to burn and are prepared to buy something else to fill the spot in the garden sooner rather than later. So what follows is the advice of experts who know and love plants and how to nurture them.

Allium wallichii

This is a clump forming flowering perennial which will do well in a sunny spot. I enjoy them because they flower for weeks!

Sue Says: "This is a plant we have been growing for several years now and I cannot understand why it is not more available to gardeners. It is of the onion family, producing lovely rounded heads of purple flowers that last for weeks and weeks to give a magnificent display. Even the seed heads in the frost are beautiful."

Aster x frikartii 'Monch' and Aster amellus 'Veilchenkonigin'

Aster x frikartii 'Monch'

I love Asters! For a start there are so many different types to choose from and they come in various hues, some of which are really good for flower decoration. I also love Asters because to me they are old fashioned and they remind me of my dad. It is always a good idea to plant something in the garden that brings back happy memories. There again, they remind me of Nick because he is old fashioned!

Nick Says: "I would agree to having been fashioned, but old? Aster x frikartii 'Monch' is a fantastic plant that would always have a very special place in any of my gardens. Not only does it produce masses of beautiful, rich lavender-blue, large daisy-like flowers continuously from July to October but it's also mildew resistant! Aster amellus 'Veilchenkonigin' (or Violet Queen to us normal folk) is a beautiful shorter variety, with the deep violet flowers having yellow centres and only reaching 30cm (12"), so it is a good one to look down on! It also has the added bonus of being mildew resistant, which is some consolation I suppose for such an unpronounceable name."

Astilbe 'Ellie van Veen', Astilbe chinensis 'Purpurkerze' and Astilbe 'Fanal'

Astilbe can also be used as a cut flower but they don't last too long, however when the flower heads die off on the plant they make an attractive autumnal show in the garden. Remember to divide the plants every three or four years to keep them growing and flowering at their best.

Sue Says: "It is sometimes quite difficult to get a pure, clean white flower in the garden which is why I like Astilbe 'Ellie van Veen' so much. It produces numerous large, fluffy plumes during June and July that reach about 60cm (24") over a clump of lovely fresh green leaves.

Astilbe chinensis 'Purpurkerze' is a plant that I put into a border to really liven it up, with its vibrant purple-rose flowers standing proudly above a good clump of green leaves.

Astilbe 'Fanal' is another variety that seems to have it all, as it is an excellent flowerer with stunning crimson-red plumes and lovely glossy, green leaves that have reddish undertones. All of these varieties will do equally well in semi-shade or shade growing in most soil types and will even take the sun in a bog garden."

Astilbe 'Fanal'

Astilbe chinensis 'Purpurkerze'

Astrantia major 'Ruby Wedding'

Another clump forming perennial that will thrive in a woodland garden or in a moist border. Keep the flower heads for dried flower decorations.

Sue Says: "A plant that always seems as if it should be much more difficult to grow than it is, don't ask me why but that is the way it seems to me! Although John is correct in that this plant will grow in a light woodland aspect it is also just as much at home in full sun. The dark red flowers are produced on 60cm (24") stiff, red-tinged green stems from April to July, although if you are lucky you should get a second flush of flowers late on in the season. Even after the first flush of flowers have gone the clump of dark green leaves act as an excellent foil for other plants around it. The other great thing about this plant is that it saves all that worry about what to buy friends and relatives for their ruby wedding anniversary!"

Callicarpa bodinieri giraldii 'Profusion'

These species of evergreen shrubs are often grown for their highly coloured fruit, which occur more in a long, hot summer. Plant them in clusters to encourage pollination and more fruit.

Sue Says: "John is right in what he says but we get berries on our magnificent Callicarpa every year and anyway John, when was the last time we had a long hot summer? This one can be slow to get going but is most definitely worth waiting for. It grows in sun or semi-shade and is not really noticeable for most of the year, not even when it produces masses of small pink flowers, but once the leaves have dropped, WOW! The bare branches are clothed with tight bunches of the most amazing deep metallic, lilac-purple berries that last for a long time after leaf fall. Visitors to the gardens really cannot believe these berries are real and one lady left still insisting that we had glued these artificial balls in place!"

Campanula lactiflora, Campanula lactiflora 'Prichard's Variety' and Campanula lactiflora 'Loddon Anna'

The basic colour of this huge family of plants is blue but you will also see white and pink versions and what's more there are varieties to suit many different positions in the garden. A plant to please all!

Campanula lactiflora 'Loddon Anna'

Nick Says: "I've gone for the lactiflora types as they not only give invaluable height to a border but they will grow in sun or semi-shade and give a spectacular flowering display all through the summer and often into autumn. I really couldn't split these three types so have included them all.

Campanula lactiflora is the species and has such a delicate pale blue flower, held in clusters to produce a large head at the top of stiff stems, which usually reach about 120cm (48"). The one drawback of all three varieties is that they produce so much flower that the stems sometimes have the tendency to flop, so we always support ours just in case.

Campanula lactiflora 'Prichard's Variety' is violet-blue in colour and in the evening light the flower heads really glow.

Campanula lactiflora 'Loddon Anna' is a lovely dusky-pink."

Chrysanthemum 'Cottage Apricot'

Another 'old favourite'! I just love the somewhat musty smell of Chrysanths and they also remind me of my youth when my brother George told me that we would make our fortune growing cuttings in the garage. It is true that you can easily grow these wonderful plants yourself but the bit about making a fortune is just not true.

Nick Says: "Chrysanths have been popular for years because they provide invaluable late summer and autumn colour. This variety is no exception. It produces masses of large bronze-apricot, daisy-like flowers on stems that reach 60cm (24"). It is a variety that will really warm the cockles of your heart on those cold autumn mornings."

Clematis tangutica and Clematis 'Royal Velvet'

Just about any one of the over two hundred species of this wonderful climber will grace any garden but there are pitfalls for the beginner. Pruning and cutting back varies so always check with the experts (or ask Nick) before you get to work with the cutters.

Nick Says: "Firstly, ignore John's 'cutting' remark. Even with the higher risk of Clematis wilt I wouldn't be put off having them in my garden. I have chosen two types to fill some more awkward positions. The rampant climber tangutica produces masses of pendant, yellow, lantern-like flowers during the summer which are followed by stunning fluffy seed heads that look good when gently blowing in the breeze or covered in frost. 'Royal Velvet' is a more controlled climber and will also grow in sun or shade. If planted in a sunny spot they like their roots cool and in the shade so it's a good idea to plant around the base or cover the ground with slate or stones. I like this variety growing up and through trees, although it is just as good on fencing or walls. Remember to cut the large flowered varieties back to about 20cm (8") from the ground each February if you are growing them on a wall or fence as they flower on the current year's wood, this keeps the flowers at a viewable height and stops the lower stems becoming bare."

Clematis 'Royal Velvet'

Clerodendrum trichotomum fargesii

A nice bushy shrub with bronze young leaves and flowers with maroon sepals. Just so that you know, the dictionary definition of sepal is: 'One of the usually green segments forming the calyx of a flower' (I didn't know that either!).

Sue Says: "You know it never ceases to amaze me how little John does actually know! Remember what I said about the Callicarpa berries? This plant produces berries as well and most definitely has that WOW factor. Not only are the drooping flowers much

more noticeable but they are also fragrant and appear late in the season, usually for August and September. These are followed by lovely autumn colours at leaf fall and then coloured berries that literally take your breath away. The clusters of small aquamarine-blue berries stop you in your tracks and stay on the bush for several weeks. It is ideally suited to a sunny position in a soil that does not dry out too much where it will slowly reach 4-6m (12'-20')."

Corylus avellana 'Contorta'

With twisted stems for winter interest and catkins in early spring I can understand why this plant is a favourite of many gardeners.

Sue Says: "This is a shrub that I would have in any garden and the one we have at Barnsdale is now 2.5m (8') high and fully grown. It is viewed in awe by every visitor that passes it and is impossible to miss

from late autumn through to early summer. We grow this plant for the sheer beauty of its stems, they curl dramatically in all directions, to create a mesmerising display. There is an added bonus with this plant, in winter you can cut a few stems and stand them in an empty vase to create a simple but very effective arrangement."

Deschampsia flexuosa 'Tatra Gold'

I must admit to not being familiar with this grass, but the way Nick describes it I'll have to buy at least one next time I'm up at Barnsdale, it sounds terrific and I think I might just have the ideal pot for it.

Nick Says: "I must say that I have a love hate relationship with grasses, but this is a variety that I definitely love. It is so bright in the spring with its narrow yellow leaves brightening even the dullest day and these leaves will keep most of that brightness throughout the year. Then during April the clump is topped by an abundance of delicate, bronze-tinted flowers that gently sway in the breeze. This surely is an evergreen that should grace the front of at least one border in everyone's garden or a pot on the patio."

Eryngium x variifolium

You can use these plants to help in a 'naturalized' area of your garden and place them in flower arrangements as well. If you are going to use them in a vase it is best to cut the stems before the flowers are completely open.

Sue Says: "Sometimes it is very hard to narrow a whole group of plants down to just one variety and I was categorically told I could only have one – life is so unfair! These are great plants because in the spring most of them belie the beauty about to unfold. The basal rosette of leaves is pretty boring but in early summer the flower spikes begin to explode upwards. The silvery-blue flower cones are surrounded by a lethal-looking, silver frill. They like to be grown in a sunny and well drained site and do well by the sea, as their common name plainly suggests – where else would you grow sea holly? They must also have caviar-like nectar because the amount of insects visiting for their fill in one day is quite staggering, so these are a must for any wildlife friendly garden, Mediterranean garden, seaside garden – well, any garden really."

Euphorbia griffithii 'Fireglow' and Euphorbia polychroma

Strange to relate but I only really discovered Euphorbia when I started visiting Barnsdale and these days I notice them everywhere. I should have spotted them before really because there are over two thousand species! Be a little careful because contact with the sap of this plant can cause irritation to the skin.

Euphorbia griffithii 'Fireglow'

Sue Says: "If you are looking for your money's worth both these varieties of Euphorbia will give you that, they are interesting from the minute the shoots poke through the ground in spring. Euphorbia griffithii 'Fireglow' emerges with a most wonderful red colour and grows up like beetroot coloured asparagus. Once the leaves have uncurled the shoots can reach 80cm (32"). They take on a more red-green colour and are then topped by wonderfully contrasting and complementary brick red flowers. We have it growing happily in sun and semi-shade and it will tolerate almost any soil type.

Euphorbia polychroma will grow in any garden soil and it will also tolerate sun or semi-shade. The lovely narrow, small leaves appear in early spring with their spectacular green colouring to lighten up even the dullest of spots, but this is eclipsed once they have achieved their 45cm (18") yearly growth as they are topped by heads of large bright yellow flowers that act as a solar explosion. This is a valuable plant for reliable early spring colour year in, year out."

Euphorbia polychroma

Exochorda giraldii wilsonii

Lots of showy white flowers on this plant that you can use in a border or as a specimen plant. It appears not to encourage any real pests either which, in an organic garden, is helpful.

Nick Says: "Any Exochorda will give a lovely, clean display of white in the spring, but this particular variety has larger flowers than most, although it does produce slightly fewer of them, so all in all the effect is about the same. I particularly like this one because it gets up to about 3m (10') and makes a real statement in a sunny position, although we have it in dappled shade and it is still performing magnificently."

Geranium 'Tanya Rendall'

My old dad called them 'Pelagorams', he meant Pelargoniums but either way he was wrong. It doesn't matter because they are simply wonderful (and dad did grow a mean one even if he wasn't sure what he was growing).

Sue Says: "This new variety was launched by us in 2005 at the Gardeners' World Live Exhibition at the NEC in Birmingham and what a beauty it is. It was bred in the Orkneys so is as tough as they come and flowers continuously right through the summer and into the autumn. The flowers are small but produced in abundance and they make a spectacular show. They are bright reddish-purple with a white eye that makes them leap off the bed of dark purple-green leaves beneath. They will also grow in sun or semi-shade in most soil types, reaching a maximum height of about 15cm (6")."

Geum 'Lionel Cox'

Grow these plants, which form large clumps, to enjoy in your garden and to split and share with your gardening friends.

Nick Says: "This is an easy to grow plant that will brighten the front of any border during spring and early summer. The abundance of creamy-yellow, saucer-shaped flowers will reach about 30cm (12") on sturdy stems, above a clump of fresh green leaves. From an easily obtainable genus of plants I have chosen a not so common variety, but in my opinion one of the best."

Gunnera manicata

Barnsdale has so many 'stars' but this plant literally stands head and shoulders above many. In early summer you can see the greenish-red flowers but the true splendour of this plant are the leaves.

Sue Says: "This plant alone is reason enough for anybody to build themselves a bog garden because it will give structure and beauty to any moisture retentive area. The flowers appear, cone shaped, in spring from the centre of the plant and before the leaves are large enough to hide them. The leaves themselves are of interest from the moment they begin to emerge and unfurl in the spring right through the season. Once the massive, thorny leaves have come to the end they should be cut off, upturned and placed over the crown to give extra winter insulation and something different to look at. The 2-2.5m (6'-8') leaves will also make an excellent shelter if you are caught in the garden during a short sharp shower."

Helianthus 'Lemon Queen'

With its dark green leaves and pale yellow florets this plant is a sight to behold from late summer to early autumn but then who doesn't like sunflowers?

Nick Says: "It never ceases to amaze me how the sunflower and its relatives hold such a special place in the hearts of British gardeners and this variety is no exception. The flowers emerge just as most things in the garden are starting to look tired, after several weeks of hot sunny weather and, of course, the flowers replace the fading sun to give invaluable light to late summer and autumn borders."

Helleborus orientalis

This is one for mid-winter or spring when it produces white or greenish-cream flowers which become pinkish with age. (Remember there is always something to see at Barnsdale, even in winter.)

Sue Says: "This plant can be relied upon to produce an excellent burst of colour during winter and spring. You can enhance the colours by cutting back the previous year's leaves as the buds appear. As flowering is coming to an end you will already have new leaves unfurling that will be green and glossy throughout the year. We find that, short of paying the earth for a named hybrid, the best colours are obtained from your own seedlings, so when you find seedlings growing around your plant always leave a few and hope for something special. You will find that the flowers' colours range from white through to pink through to a deep purple that is almost black, some being spotted. There are single flowers through to doubles and all the various combinations between! The possibilities are endless. The one downside, literally, is that the flowers hang downwards so they are seen at their best whilst resting in a prostrate position looking up to the sky!"

Hemerocallis 'Elegant Candy', 'Big Smile', 'Siloam Justin Lee' and 'Longfields Twins'

Known as the Day Lily, these evergreen or semi-evergreen plants enjoy well drained soil and can be grown in a mixed or herbaceous border. Some varieties only flower for one day, others open late afternoon and flower at night. You might like to impress your neighbours with the word 'remontant' meaning 'flowering repeatedly'.

Sue says: "These are a real passion of mine and so far I have collected over 300 different varieties, although I keep telling Nick that this is nowhere near enough as there are over 40,000 different varieties to choose from. I am still waiting for a printable reply!

All the varieties I have chosen have trumpet-shaped flowers and will grow in sun or semi-shade.

'Siloam Justin Lee'

'Elegant Candy' is simply gorgeous, the rounded, pink flowers have a red eye and contrasting yellow throat.

'Big Smile' has an enormous yellow flower with delicately ruffled bluish-pink edges. An absolute must for any garden.

'Siloam Justin Lee' is a real winner with its reflexed, rounded purple-red petals and yellow-green throat.

'Elegant Candy'

'Longfields Twins' has large, double rust red flowers that have a yellow halo and erratic yellow highlights. It is definitely one of those flowers you have to stop and have a really good, close look at."

'Big Smile'   'Longfields Twins'

Hesperis matronalis 'Alba'

Insects love this plant, it's a pretty short-lived variety but well worth the effort.

Nick Says: "Another classic cottage garden plant that surely must have a place in any garden for its perfume alone. This early summer flowerer always turns heads, as most people cannot work out where the beautiful perfume is emanating from and they are usually surprised to find that it is from this plant! Although beautiful, the flowers do not necessarily stand out in a border but they do tend to set off plants around them and at 60-90cm (24-36") high they are easy to cope with. It will gently seed around and usually find its own best spot, so even if your original plant is short-lived you will never be without at least one in your garden."

Heuchera 'Chocolate Ruffles', Heuchera 'Obsidian', Heuchera 'Ebony and Ivory' and Heuchera 'Caramel'

It was Sue who introduced me to Heucheras and I will be forever grateful because these wonderful plants can be used in so many ways. I began by planting several different varieties alongside each other in a 'Heuchera bed' and the result was splendid. Sue then suggested that I should try them in containers and well, I'll let her tell you about them.

Heuchera 'Obsidian'

Sue says: "In recent years there has been an upsurge in Heuchera breeding and many excellent varieties have become available, here are four suggestions.

Heuchera 'Chocolate Ruffles' produces an excellent clump of large, evergreen purple-maroon leaves with chocolate coloured tips, topped by a fabulous display of cream coloured flowers. During winter, on a frosty morning the wavy leaf edges give a sugary effect that makes them almost good enough to eat.

Heuchera 'Obsidian' is one of the newer varieties. It has beautiful dark, shiny leaves and creamy coloured flowers. This is one of the shorter varieties, with the flowers only reaching 25cm (10") in height.

Heuchera 'Ebony and Ivory' is a lovely variety and it often causes people to stop and admire the large ivory-white flowers which can reach 45cm (18") together with the beautiful bright ebony coloured leaves.

My final choice is also a new variety called Heuchera 'Caramel'. The caramel coloured, undulating leaves tend not to scorch in the sun. You can use it to brighten up a shady or dull area. The white flowers are produced during the summer and will reach approximately 25cm (10") in height."

Heuchera 'Chocolate Ruffles'

Hosta 'Sum and Substance' and Hosta 'Hydon Sunset'

I love them, Sue loves them, Nick loves them and unfortunately slugs love them! Hostas like cool, shady positions where they can 'show off'. With veined and lacquered leaves they are particularly well suited to shady areas and can be used very effectively in conjunction with a plethora of shade-loving plants.

Hosta 'Sum and Substance'

Sue Says: "Hosta 'Sum and Substance' is an excellent spot plant that I have chosen because it is bold and has the most enormous greenish-yellow leaves that bring to life any dull, damp area. In July the pale lavender flowers explode like a firework display from the centre of this spectacular clump. Hosta 'Hydon Sunset' is a fantastic small-leaved Hosta that will produce a clump about 60-90cm (24-36") across. We have it in shade, although it will also grow in semi-shade, and the bright yellow leaves brighten what would otherwise have been a bit of a dank and dreary spot. It also has lavender coloured flowers which contrast superbly with the leaves."

Hosta 'Hydon Sunset'

Iris sibirica and Iris x robusta 'Gerald Darby'

My dad called them 'flags' and he wasn't far wrong with that description. There are some three hundred species and many of them make wonderful cut flowers. Others simply look great at what they do best, grace any garden.

Nick Says: "There are many different varieties of Iris sibirica to choose from and it is always hard to find just one or two to write about. However, the species which, we are told, has been superseded by supposedly better varieties and largely forgotten about by modern day gardeners, is one of my favourites. An easy to grow variety, although they all benefit from a bit of moisture retention, which loves the sun and will satisfy even the most impatient of gardeners with the speed it produces a decent clump. The spikes of blue-purple, beardless flowers are massed at the tops of stiff stems and are at their best late on when they glow in the evening light.

Iris x robusta 'Gerald Darby' is a stunning plant, with a long period of interest which starts as soon as the leaves appear in spring. From beneath the cold ground emerge the dark violet tinged green leaves, which keep their colour through the early part of the season and end with mainly purple spotting at the base. The blue-violet flowers emerge in June at the tops of dark violet stems, which gives a beautiful contrast.

Both these varieties will grow to between 75 and 120cm (30"-48") and will probably need dividing about every 5 years or so to keep the clump vigorous and flowering at its best."

Iris sibirica

Iris x robusta 'Gerald Darby'

Leptinella potentillina

There are some thirty species of Leptinella and mostly they are best used as low ground cover or in between paving.

Sue Says: "I'm sorry but I just cannot get liverwort out of my head when thinking of this plant. It is mainly grown for its ferny, evergreen leaves that take on bronze hues in the winter and its very low creeping habit which makes it an ideal plant for walls, crevices, between paving or just in an alpine feature. But I love it for the insignificant liverwort-like flowers produced in the spring, because they give off the most unexpected honey smell. It is quite amazing to watch our garden visitors smelling all the plants around this one to see where the scent is coming from as it seems impossible that such a small flower could emit such a strong odour."

Leycesteria formosa

Most suitable in a woodland garden, these plants have hollow, cane-like stems.

Nick Says: "We mainly grow these in sunny positions, but also have some in semi-shade and they do equally well. To get the best from this plant it is vital to cut about a third of it back very hard in the spring to revitalize it, otherwise over time it will get woody and not perform at its best. The drooping panicles of white flowers, surrounded by claret bracts, gradually begin to hang down from June and these flowers are then followed in early September by lovely large purple berries, giving a very long season of interest. This is an easy to grow plant that, in the right situation, will reach about 1.8m (6')."

Lonicera etrusca 'Michael Rosse' and Lonicera involucrata

It is easy to get confused with Lonicera because most people think of honeysuckle as a climber but there are a number of shrubby varieties, some of which can be used as ground cover plants. You can plant honeysuckle at almost any time of the year and they are tolerant of most soils.

Sue Says: "'Michael Rosse' is an absolute must for any garden, balcony, courtyard, fence, pergola or in fact just about anywhere. This less common variety, in my opinion, is the best honeysuckle both for the colour of its creamy-yellow flowers, which cover the plant in early summer, and the amazing scent they exude, especially in the evening. The reddish stems and grey-green leaves enhance the flowers and give interest well after the blooms have gone.

I cannot understand why Lonicera involucrata is not much better known. I mean, what more could you want than a shrub that is as

tough as old boots, grows in sun or semi-shade, in any soil type, flowers and even has berries to follow? Fantastic! It is an upright shrub that in June produces masses of yellow flowers surrounded by two distinct red bracts. The bracts stay in place while the yellow flowers are replaced by shiny black berries."

Lonicera etrusca 'Michael Rosse'

Lychnis coronaria

I've got this in my garden and it gently seeds around so even if I lose my main plant I always have another to fall back onto. Even in my poor soil, in full sun it does fantastically.

Sue Says: "There are some plants that catch the eye in whatever situation they are put into and this variety definitely fits that bill. The clump of grey leaves will stay evergreen throughout most winters with the rose-crimson flowers held on stiff stems that will reach about 60cm (24") in a sunny spot."

Lysimachia punctata 'Alexander'

A genus of approximately one hundred and fifty species of herbaceous and evergreen perennials and shrubs. They mainly like damp areas of grassland and woodland.

Nick Says: "A variety that looks good from the minute it pokes its head above ground until it starts to die back in late autumn. The many tiny shoot heads emerge a vibrant pinky-red in early spring before the leaves turn greener with a cream variegation, although if you plant in a drier area it is possible to get some pink to stay in the leaf. Then in summer these upright stems are topped by masses of bright yellow flowers that contrast superbly with the leaves. It is a reasonably vigorous clump-former that does best in a sunny position in most soil types."

Miscanthus sinensis 'Nippon' and Molinia caerulea 'Edith Dudszus'

Many gardeners choose to plant ornamental grasses these days and I am one of them. As a young gardener I wouldn't have dreamt of such a thing but there are so many different plants to choose from. See what Nick and Sue have achieved at Barnsdale when you visit.

Sue Says: "Miscanthus sinensis 'Nippon' is a plant for late summer and autumn. From an erect clump of long, narrow green leaves its flowers, with fabulous red-tinged plumes gently sway in the breeze. But the interest doesn't stop there. We never cut back the 45-90cm (18"-36") of top growth as it is a fabulous host for frost and the harder the frost the more spectacular it looks, particularly with the mid morning sun just starting to filter through. There's also a range of grasses that have more typically grass-like flowers and Molinia caerulea 'Edith Dudszus' is one. The lovely open panicles of rich purple flowers are produced in autumn at the tops

of dark red-purple stems. Another that gets to about 90 cm (36"), plant in a position where it catches the breeze to get those beautiful flowers swaying."

Miscanthus sinensis 'Nippon'

Omphalodes cappadocica 'Starry Eyes'

Watch out for the slugs if you choose to grow these clump-forming plants. They quite like partial shade (the plants that is, not the slugs) and reward you with white-eyed blue flowers in early spring.

Sue Says: "This plant has something rather special in store when it flowers in the spring. The masses of small blue flowers open with a very distinct pale pink edge to give a staggeringly beautiful display to the front of the border. An easy to grow plant in a difficult position, it will only reach 25cm (10") in height."

Ophiopogon planiscapus 'Nigrescens'

Evergreen perennials which sometimes have fleshy swollen roots, but beware! Slugs may cause damage to the leaves but that's all part of organic gardening.

Sue Says: "I can understand why people get confused when they try to classify this evergreen perennial and usually mark it down as a grass, especially when you consider it is commonly known as 'the black grass'. It is however, a perennial and I use it as one of my most valuable all year round plants, not only in the border but also in containers on the ground and hanging on walls. As if the black leaves are not enough, it also produces delicate purple-white flowers on short stems that are followed by black berries and it is quite happy in sun or semi-shade in most garden soils. Each year it will produce a slightly larger clump and reach about 20cm in height."

Osteospermum 'Mary'

With their simple daisy-like flowers Osteospermum are most pleasing to the eye and offer late spring to early autumn colour in any border.

Nick Says: "This variety is a tender perennial, but I have chosen it because it has the most striking deep purple flowers that have a complementary blue eye. Perfect for a sunny border or container, it will flower and flower until the first frosts when it will need to be brought in and protected until the early summer. It needs a bit of TLC through the winter, but it's well worth the effort for the non-stop summer display. There is an easy way to tell if your Osteospermum is tender or hardy because all upright varieties are tender whilst most prostrate varieties are hardy in a sunny and well drained position."

Panicum virgatum 'Heavy Metal'

Another wonderful grass, it has metallic blue-grey leaves that turn yellow in autumn. I am tempted to suggest that maybe another type could be named 'Don't Panicum Mr Mainwaring' but I wouldn't do that!

Sue Says: "When I first met John his jokes were bad, but I never thought that even he could stoop as low as that, particularly when talking about such a fabulous plant. I have to admit to loving grasses and this is one of my favourites, mainly because of the loose heads of purple-green flowers that blow gently back and forth in the wind to such an amazing effect. However, once the flowers have gone over and the autumn leaf colours have faded this plant has a second wind. We leave the top growth on so that after a cold night you come out to a fantastic frosty specimen that could compete with any bright flower for beauty. Best when grown in a sunny, open position, this variety will reach about 90cm (36") in height."

Penstemon varieties

They thrive in a well drained soil and will grow in sun or semi-shade, often producing unusual colours. Penstemon are very useful in the garden because most varieties flower from early June right through into the autumn and they come in various heights. They perform best in well drained soils and may be short-lived in heavier clay soils.

Nick Says: "I love Penstemon and have so far collected over 150 different varieties. I like them so much because they are such good value for money. Penstemon come in a range of colours and heights to suit every situation. I suppose that I have to say that with its lovely wine-red translucent flowers, Penstemon 'Geoff Hamilton' is one of my favourites. It was bred by two very good friends, Clive and Kathy Gandley, who are holders of one of the National Collections of Penstemon. Clive and Kathy named this plant in memory of my father not long after his death. He was also a great fan of this plant and we have many different varieties planted in the gardens. Other favourites are 'Alice Hindley', which has large lilac and white flowers on a plant that reaches 120cm (48"), as does 'Rosy Blush' which has large rose-pink and white flowers. 'Raven' is one of the darkest purple varieties, whilst 'Osprey' has large white flowers with a distinct pink front and both are probably easier to position in the border as they only get up to 60cm (24"). I could go on forever, but will finish by mentioning when to cut them back and where to grow them, as this seems to be an area that a lot of Penstemonites don't really understand. The varieties that grow over 90cm (36") only have the old flower spikes cut back after flowering and never further than that, whilst all the other upright varieties are cut back hard, to within 10cm (4") of the base, in mid to late April. This will prevent the base becoming woody and revitalise the plant to give you even more flowers every season! As they dislike the winter wet, a well drained soil is preferable and we have them growing perfectly happily in both sun and semi-shade."

Penstemon 'Rosy Blush'

Penstemon 'Charles Rudd'

Penstemon hartwegii 'Albus'

Penstemon 'Raven'

Penstemon 'Willys Purple'

Penstemon 'Alice Hindley'

Penstemon 'Rosy Blush'

Phytolacca americana

Found in open fields and woodland in Africa and Asia, these plants have good-looking foliage but they do not smell good! The fruit can be lethal if eaten so do not plant where children may have access.

Nick Says: "I don't just like this plant because it looks quite rude, I picked it because it is not all that common and has a long period of interest, drawing the attention of visitors from late spring until late autumn. It is a very adaptable plant that is equally at home in either sun or shade and will very often gently seed itself in a position it likes, better than the one you've put it in! The green leaves emerge with faint pink tinges and then in early summer the white flowers open, often pink flushed, on tall, cylindrical spikes. The flowers then give way to green berries that gradually change colour until they become the most fantastic shiny, purple-black mass. I suppose the easiest way to describe them in this state is as a black corn-on-the-cob and we actually had a visitor ask us if they were ready for harvest, but in fact the berries would not do you much good and the root, which looks like a cross between a sweet potato and a carrot, is poisonous."

Potentilla fruticosa 'Red Robin' and Potentilla 'Flamenco'

The first shrub I ever bought was a Potentilla and I still love them. I have to say that I prefer those with the simple yellow flowers but in truth, no garden is complete without at least one of these.

Nick Says: "I also love the shrubby Potentillas, because they are one of those plants that you can do almost anything with and each year they will come back bigger and better than the last. Potentilla 'Red Robin' will get up to anywhere between 60-90cm (24"-36"), but it does like a good trim in the winter to tidy it up and keep it nice and compact, as do all the Potentilla fruticosa varieties. I usually attack ours with a pair of shears! 'Red Robin' is quite obviously red, but rarely called Robin! It is the best red variety, in my opinion, as it stays red and doesn't fade to orange."

Sue Says: "Potentilla 'Flamenco', what an eye catcher! I love hot colours and the almost velvet, bright crimson, saucer-shaped flowers, produced in abundance by this plant, certainly fit the bill. It flowers all summer on stems that will reach up to 60cm (24") and as the season progresses the flowers age to bright orange, almost setting your border on fire! The clump of strawberry-like green leaves will invariably stay evergreen all through the milder winters."

Potentilla 'Flamenco'

Primula double forms

Too many different varieties to describe here but you can be certain that Sue has chosen some great ones for you.

Sue Says: "I cannot understand why these plants are not grown more widely as they give such a good burst of colour in early spring with, if you are lucky, a second flowering in the autumn. Typically only reaching 15cm (6") in height, there are a number of lovely specimens to choose from but my particular favourites are 'Dawn Ansell' which is a pure white, 'Marie Crousse' having violet flowers that are laced with ivory and 'Blue Sapphire' producing masses of vivid blue flowers. All will grow in sun or shade in a moisture retentive soil."

Primula 'Marie Crousse'

Primula 'Dawn Ansell'

Pulmonaria saccharata 'Samurai' and Pulmonaria angustifolia azurea

These are good in woodland areas and with their attractive leaves and flowers they look good in a border as well. In addition, bees love them.

Nick Says: "I think it must tell you something when I keep listing hard to kill plants! These plants definitely fall into that category and can be left to their own devices and will perform well every year.

Pulmonaria saccharata 'Samurai' is a fantastic variety that produces purple-blue flowers during April-May above a good clump of completely silver leaves and, because this variety is evergreen, the leaves will add unusual interest to your garden all year round.

Pulmonaria angustifolia azurea is the other variety I have chosen, it is deciduous and after flowering the lush, dark green leaves provide excellent ground cover and set off flowering plants around them. However, the beauty of this plant is most definitely in its flowers, which are the most magnificent rich blue, and in the evening light or on duller spring days they glow and will light up any dark corner. It will tolerate most soil conditions and we have them growing in the gardens in dense shade and semi-shade with most varieties being around 30cm (12") in height."

Pulmonaria angustifolia azurea

Ribes sanguineum 'Red Pimpernel' and Ribes sanguineum 'White Icicle'

You can grow these in an informal hedge or in the shrubbery and if you like, you can simply call them a 'flowering currant' (as my dad did).

Sue Says: "It is always nice to have something a little bit different than the norm in the garden and both these varieties fit into that category. Ribes sanguineum 'Red Pimpernel' is a darker red, almost crimson, than the usual varieties offered and really stands out amongst all the other emerging foliage during the spring.

I like Ribes sanguineum 'White Icicle' because it not only reminds me of the weather that has just passed, hopefully, but also because it is one of the hardier white varieties. Both will grow in sun or semi-shade and reach about 180cm (6') in height if you let them, but we always prune ours after flowering to keep the flowers down to a comfortable viewing height."

Ribes sanguineum 'White Icicle'

Ribes sanguineum 'Red Pimpernel'

Rodgersia podophylla

Creamy-green flowers and purplish young leaves - this is a winner.

Nick Says: "I have to admit to being the sort of gardener who doesn't have to see flowers on a plant for it to be interesting. That said, this particular plant does flower and it is beautiful in its own right being 100cm (40") high, creamy-green and fluffy, although I grow this one for its gorgeous horse chestnut-like leaves. They emerge in spring, a succulent bronze colour, then gradually turn a more bronze-green as the season progresses, before a final burst of bronze-red in autumn. A superb plant for a position in sun or semi-shade, but do be warned because the more sun you give it the more moisture it will require at the root, to prevent scorching of those fabulous leaves."

Rosa 'Blush Noisette'

I know that this plant is a favourite of Nick's so Sue can tell you all about it!

Sue Says: "A delicate flower of small proportions but very big in the beauty and scent stakes. The small semi-double lilac pink, noisette flowers are produced in abundance from June right through until the frosts. It is not a tall or vigorous climber, only reaching about 4.5m (13'), but we have it on an arch and for most of the season you cannot see the foliage for the amount of flowers. You would have thought that would be ample for any plant but then when you get closer to it you are suddenly overcome by a strong clove scent, to the amazement of most garden visitors."

Rubus spectabilis 'Olympic Double'

With three palmate leaves, upright, slightly prickly shoots and its double purple-pink flowers this is another candidate for the 'show off' section.

Sue Says: "I like a surprise and this plant certainly provides that in the spring when it is covered in flowers. Most people are put off Rubus because of its suckering habit but it is easily kept under control with a spade once a year. The drawbacks are vastly outweighed by the sheer unexpected beauty of the large, fragrant, double pink-maroon flowers that cover the plant. It is an easy to grow plant for sun or semi-shade, in any soil type that deserves a place in any border. The only word of warning I would give is to beware when digging up the suckers as they are mighty prickly because they are related to the raspberry and blackberry."

Rudbeckia fulgida sullivantii 'Goldsturm'

Rudbeckia originate from the meadows and woodlands of North America and they come as annuals, biennials and perennials. Slugs may damage the young growth so make sure you take a look at our 'Buglife' section!

Nick Says: "This plant is an absolute must for any garden, you can take my word for it. During the second half of the summer the bright yellow, daisy-like flowers begin to unfold from their tight buds to produce a heart stopping display right through until the

frosts. We have one planted in the gardens right in front of the purple-leaved Berberis thunbergii 'Rose Glow' which looks very pretty with its marbled new growth, but when the Rudbeckia comes into flower it has a whole new lease of life and actually makes the Rudbeckia even more noticeable, if such a thing were possible. It must have a sunny spot, to see it at its best, where it will grow up to about 60-90cm (24"-36") and it doesn't seem to be too fussy about the soil type."

Sarcococca ruscifolia

This is another one for the winter months when clusters of white fragrant flowers are produced and, not content with that, dark red fruit follows.

Sue Says: "The outstanding feature of this plant is its fantastic winter scent so it's vital that it is planted in a part of the garden that you visit in the winter months. Most visitors to Barnsdale cannot believe that such a powerful scent can be produced by such delicate white flowers. It is evergreen with the glossy green leaves producing an excellent foil for other plants in the spring and summer, with red berries produced during late summer. An easy plant for sun or shade and compact to boot, only reaching about 90cm (36") in height."

Saxifraga 'Rubrifolia'

The genus Saxifraga are mostly cushion forming and can be evergreen, semi evergreen or deciduous perennials, biennials or annuals, so surprise me Nick!

Nick Says: "This variety certainly surprised me, because until I saw it, I was under the impression that Saxifrages were generally crusty-leaved or green-leaved and cushion forming, low growing and producing saucer-shaped flowers. How wrong I was! The fortunei varieties of Saxifraga, of which this is one, are hardy perennial plants that have large, usually coloured, fleshy leaves. This variety will emerge in spring with lovely glossy red leaves to delight you for the whole summer. Then in early autumn the narrow petalled white flowers appear just above the leaves, like white peaks on the red sea! A terrific plant for the front of a border or in the rock garden as it only gets 45cm (18") high and will grow well in either shade or semi-shade."

Sedum kamtschaticum floriferum 'Weihenstephaner Gold'

Excellent plants for dry areas as they are very tolerant of drought conditions.

Sue Says; "What a range of Sedums there are and I think that this is one of the best. It is part of a range of varieties that are very well suited to alpine features, although they are just as at home at the front of a border. The small, glossy green leaves are there all year round, taking on reddish tints in the winter, but acting as the perfect foil for the star-shaped, summer-long, bright yellow flowers."

Smilacina racemosa

They need to be sheltered from the wind but are worth the effort.

Nick Says: "Having to be sheltered from the wind is not a problem for this plant as it much prefers a woodland aspect where it will, of course, be protected by the surrounding trees. Ideal for a neutral to acid soil, with the fragrant white flowers produced in April and May on arching, terminal sprays about 75cm (30") above the ground. The flowers are followed later in the season by purple-spotted, red berries which appear before the autumn when the green leaves turn wonderful shades of yellow."

Thalictrum delavayi 'Hewitt's Double'

With its delicate flowers and beautiful foliage, this plant is part of the Ranunculae family and although some varieties can be short lived they are well worth the effort.

Sue Says: "This plant gives me a really happy feeling every time I see it because it is so light, airy and delicate. The small, uncomplicated misty yellow flowers are produced in abundance on stiff stems that may reach 90cm (36") and it is ideal for the front or middle of a border as you can see through the fine mist of flowers to the plants beyond. Given a sunny position this plant will grace any border."

Tricyrtis formosana

Protect the young spring growth from the slugs!

Sue Says: "The common name for this plant is the 'Toad Lily' which seems a rather vulgar description of a quite delicate and exotic looking flower. In late summer and into autumn the tall, sturdy stems are topped by clusters of upward-facing light pink flowers that are purple spotted. They look as if they ought to be tender and 'molly-coddled' through the winter but they are 'as tough as old boots' and will reach 60cm (24") in most soil types in sun or semi-shade."

Thymus varieties

There are some three hundred and fifty species of this genus and I suppose that a Spurs supporter has chosen 'vulgaris'.

Nick Says: "John, as any football aficionado will be aware, the football at White Hart Lane is sometimes debatable, usually exciting, but never vulgar. Traditionally at Barnsdale we have used thymes in two places, either in the herb garden or in planting pockets in paths and patios. The first use is fairly self explanatory but look at some of the more interesting varieties such as x citriodorus 'Archers Gold' – yellow leaved: 'Doone Valley' – green leaves splashed yellow; and vulgaris 'Silver Posie' – silver variegated green leaves. All will add interest to any culinary delights you produce, although their taste is somewhat weaker than the common or garden thyme. Ornamentally we grow the lower, more ground hugging varieties such as the serpyllum types 'Pink Chintz' and 'Rainbow Falls' as well as 'Desbro' in our planting pockets, so that when you tread on them, as you inevitably will, the most wonderful scent is released. These low growing thymes will take very well to the odd squashing from great hob-nailed boots, so are ideal for paths. Even in flower most will only get to about 5cm (2") tall. I suppose that due to our recent lack of silverware in the White Hart Lane trophy cabinet you would have thought I would have picked Thymus serpyllum 'Minimalist' but, like most Spurs supporters, I am ever the optimist!"

Thymus 'Doone Valley'

Viburnum tinus

It is a laurel so you would expect it to be 'hardy'.

Nick Says: "I'm not an 'old fuddy duddy', but I am often astonished by the almost hypnotic manner in which people are seduced into believing that new plant releases are automatically better and therefore they totally disregard older, tried and tested and sometimes, much better varieties. This plant is one of those, as it has been cultivated in our gardens since the late 16th century and in 1969 was given the Award of Garden Merit by the Royal Horticultural Society. The masses of evergreen, dark green glossy leaves will set off any other plants close to it, but its true value lies in the flat cymes of pink budded, white flowers that are produced from late autumn until early spring, thus giving loads of flower interest at a difficult time of year. Having said all of that, I find the berries produced in late summer and that precede the flowers, to be of as much interest. They appear a fabulous metallic-blue colour that gradually turns black. An easy plant to keep to

whatever size you require by regular pruning and one that will grow in any position you wish to give it and even grows by the sea – now, what more could you ask for?"

Viola 'Barnsdale Gem'

Very easy to grow and once they get going they will spread and flower almost at will.

Nick Says: "Discovered by my father in the gardens at Barnsdale amongst a clump of Viola 'Ardross Gem', this mound forming variety produces masses of medium-sized, dark velvet-purple flowers that have a yellow eye. We have found that it grows well in sun or semi-shade, achieving a height of about 30cm (12") and flowers from April right through the summer."

Barnsdale's Own Gardeners' Question Time - Part 1

During the course of a year Barnsdale is visited by thousands of keen gardeners from all over the world and many of them have questions for Nick, Sue and the other members of the team. We decided to give visitors the chance to put their questions in writing so that we could include them in the book. The reasoning being that, if visitors ask questions they are probably going to be representative of what others might like to ask! Listed in this section are a selection but do continue to ask members of staff if you have a question of your own, when you next visit Barnsdale or through their website www.barnsdalegardens.co.uk.

Mrs. M. Macgregor from Arlewas. When is the best time to prune a large bay tree? It is twenty feet high and in excess of forty years old. Can it be done? Can I take a cutting and grow it on? *Well Mrs. Macgregor, by my reckoning that's three questions but here's Nick's answer.*

It's always best to prune when a tree or shrub reaches its ideal size rather than carrying out reconstructive pruning. But I realise that this is not always possible, particularly when plants are inherited with a newly purchased house. With this particular plant the best time to prune is early spring when it would usually receive a gentle clip all over. However, if more drastic pruning is required, then it needs to be spread out over a period of 2-3 years, maybe cutting back a third each time until the required size is reached. When cutting back always remember to keep an eye on how you would like the finished shape to be. Propagation is usually by semi-ripe cuttings in summer, although they can also be grown from seed.

Mrs. D. Yardley in Tarksey, Lincoln. How high does new box hedging need to be before it can be trimmed?

The answer is really as high as you like. That said, most people grow it as a low hedge and at Barnsdale we keep some of ours at 30cm (12") high and some at 45cm (18") dependant on the type of hedge we require.

Rosanne Jarvis, in Ruthin. We hear of endless methods and products to deter slugs and snails, what do you find is the ideal organic solution?

We like to use several methods because we find that different things work well in certain areas and not in others. Wood ash is an excellent deterrent, a band of this will stop slugs and snails from travelling by absorbing the mucus they need to do so. The band has to be replaced whenever it rains to ensure maximum absorption at all times. In other areas we use nematodes that we water onto the surface of the soil. These work very well, although the one big downside is that they need a regular temperature of 5 degrees centigrade in order to work, so there can be some early spring damage before you can use them. We also use organic slug pellets which are based on ferric phosphate. These are harmful to slugs and snails but not to other important wildlife, and when they break down they add vital natural nutrients to the soil. Another method of control is to use what nature provides and to have an excellent population of birds, hedgehogs, frogs, etc. in the garden to do the work for us.

Mrs. R. L. Brown Syston, Leicestershire. I have a Hydrangea Petrolaris which grows on a north facing wall but, despite never having been fed, it is taking over the house and has designs on the roof! How can I keep it under control?

The one thing that climbing Hydrangeas don't mind is being treated roughly. This includes planting it in awful soil, not feeding it and being brutal with the secateurs! Renovation pruning of this variety needs to be carried out during its dormant period, so any time during winter or early spring, just cut back the main framework to smaller side - shoots and reduce it in this way to a reasonable height. Although it will seem very harsh the plant will quickly grow back. Then, each year, make sure you prune back gently to keep it under control.

Mary Venning. What type of nuts can I grow on my allotment in **Nottingham**? I already have a hazelnut. *I'm quite sure that there are a number of nuts in Nottingham already, Mary, but here is Nick's specific answer!*

In our Country Paradise Garden we have a small but perfectly formed nut walk and this consists of a wide variety of cob nuts, all of which are growing very well and producing nuts prolifically. You could try walnuts, Juglans nigra or Juglans regia, but make sure that you buy cultivars, such as Juglans regia 'Maxima' because trees raised from seed can be very unreliable croppers. Almonds, Prunus dulcis, will also grow well in the Midlands given a sheltered and sunny spot.

Brian Reeve lives on the edge of Morecambe Bay. His garden faces west. The garden is therefore subjected to very strong, salty winds. Can you recommend some smallish trees or fast growing, colourful shrubs that will survive the harsh conditions? *I know that Sue would welcome some ideas on the subject of wind, Nick and too many brussels sprouts, Brian but here is Nick's answer to your question.*

An excellent range of varieties within the Sorbus aria and Sorbus aucuparia group of trees would really fit the bill for this spot. They are generally small trees with the aucuparia types also benefiting from flowers in the spring, berries in late summer and generally excellent autumn colours. If this does not tempt you then larger shrubs include Ilex aquifolium varieties, Viburnums, Elaeagnus varieties, and many types of Cotoneaster would also do well.

Brian Lea from Hemel Hempstead. When is the correct time to prune Wisteria?

These vigorous climbers need to be pruned twice a year. Once your framework has been established cut back all of the shoots not required to about 15cm (6") during late summer. In winter all that needs to be done is to cut back the same shoots to within 2-3 buds of the thicker, main framework stems.

Mrs. Sarah Bedding in Moulton. Does clematis grow best in pots or in the ground?

Most varieties will grow well in either. The most important requirement for Clematis is that they have their heads in the sun and their roots in the cool. So whether they are in pots or in the ground, in a sunny spot it is important to cover the soil with mulch, a large stone or a piece of slate to keep the ground cool. The more vigorous varieties are very difficult to keep going in pots but the larger flowered, summer types will do very well.

Dee Cattanach, Peterborough. Has a shady garden that is heavy clay and she wants to grow perennials and shrubs – what does Sue recommend?

The most important thing is to get as much organic matter into the soil as possible. The great thing about a clay soil is that you can manipulate it to do what you want. So if you want to grow plants that prefer good drainage then dig in plenty of organic matter and coarse grit. Or leave it for plants that prefer a heavy, wet soil such as roses. We use a lot of the David Austin English Roses in the garden as well as shrubby and perennial Potentillas, Ribes, Hemerocallis, Astilbe, Ligularia, Lonicera, honeysuckles, shrubby as well as climbing, Hostas, Geraniums, Heuchera and the list just goes on!

I. W. Torry from Goudhurst, Kent. Wants advice on growing and propagating a blueberry.

Blueberries prefer an acid soil with a pH of 4-5.5 ideally, so we have to grow ours in containers with an ericaceous compost mix. They are very easy to grow but do try to use rainwater when you give them a drink. Prune in the same way as you would blackcurrants. Propagation can be achieved by taking 10-15cm (4"-6") softwood cuttings in midsummer.

Mr. J. E. Brown in Syston. Wants to know of a reliable variety of onion seeds for the earliest sowing and when to sow (maincrop).

As any grower of vegetables knows, we all recommend what does well for us, so here goes. We have found that there is not a significant difference in maturity to make a difference. What we concentrate on is growing varieties that we like in combination with those that store well. For example we love Ailsa Craig but it does not store well so this is the first type that we eat. Lancastrian and Red Delicious have very good storage properties so these will be stored until required. If we try to get an earlier crop from one of these varieties then we will start them off, usually multi sown, in the autumn.

Lawrence Dooley in Surbiton. Is at a loss as to what his wife should do to persuade her husband to do more gardening! *Well Mr. Dooley, methinks that you know perfectly well what inducements your good lady should offer! Is it just that you are too shy to ask her?*

We find that a refusal to cook, iron, clean or the threat of selling golf clubs to a charity shop usually works. If this has been attempted and failed then one of our Barnsdale courses never ceases to inspire even the most reluctant of gardeners.

Pauline Gale from Saffron Walden. Says that she has a Yew hedge that is three years old and hasn't yet reached the required height. Should she be trimming the sides in order to thicken them?

There is definitely no point in allowing your yew hedge to grow much beyond the ultimate thickness you require. Trimming the sides will direct growth into the areas that need it, the growing tips, rather than the areas that don't. It will also help to thicken the hedge as you go, so that when the required height is achieved the hedge will already be dense.

Fiona Bashford in Horsham. Wants to know how Nick and Sue manage to fit so many trees and shrubs into the borders at Barnsdale and yet still manage to find the room for such extensive under planting.

We have always found that a combination of good plant knowledge and the desire to attempt something different usually works. That said, we have had the odd disaster! So do not be afraid to experiment, Fiona.

Gillian Silver from Ashwellthorpe, Norfolk. Wants to know if you can recommend a screening hedge with all year round interest for her country garden on heavy clay.

There are several hedging plants that do well in our Barnsdale clay, we use beech a lot. It is a very formal hedge when clipped regularly and it hangs onto its brown leaves through most of the winter. We also use quite a lot of common laurel, Prunus laurocerasus 'Rotundifolia', which has evergreen, glossy green leaves and also produces scented white flowers in spring. Its one drawback is that it needs to be pruned with secateurs because cutting with hedge trimmers leaves unsightly brown edges where the leaves have been sliced through. Thuja plicata also makes an excellent hedge with different varieties producing differing effects. The foliage, when crushed or whilst trimming, will give off a very sweet smell. Yew will also do an excellent job, although it is worth remembering that most parts are poisonous if ingested.

Mr. J. Simpson in Newport, Shropshire. How can I best avoid carrot fly in my garden in an organic way?

We have found that the use of impenetrable barriers is the best way to prevent any damage. This involves covering the crop with either horticultural fleece or enviromesh, usually from the third week of May for 3-4 weeks. We can be fairly specific in the timescale because the life cycle of the carrot fly begins around this time when the females are looking to lay their eggs next to the carrots. Once the eggs hatch the larvae eat their way into the carrots before pupating into adults. There is another life cycle later in the year but this does not usually create the same devastating effects as the first. Covering with one of the aforementioned materials prevents the females from getting to the carrots to lay their eggs. The advantage of laying fleece on a crop is that, with early crops, it will bring them on quicker because it creates a warmer microclimate. Another method is to have a low barrier, such as box hedging or a wicker fence, around the crop area.

Mrs. Shelagh Hulse in sunny Manchester. Has noticed that the Buddleja at Barnsdale is only trimmed in late February and wants to know when it is pruned really hard.

Our Buddlejas are pruned back by about half during early winter to reduce their size and prevent them rocking around in the winter winds. We do not cut them back all the way as early spring frosts can kill off any buds that have broken into growth early. We then, generally, cut them back to one or two sets of buds from the previous year's growth in late March. It has to be a balance between frost damage and not allowing the plant to put too much effort into producing growth that is only going to be removed.

C. Webster from Queniborough. Would like to know the best material to use for a new, arched pergola trellis support in an established country garden.

In an organic garden we do not use pressure treated timber, instead we rely on boron rods or organic wood preservative. For our Reclaimed Garden we managed to find a pergola made from recycled oak roof beams which was a fantastic find! These finds are few and far between but hardwoods from renewable sources will last well in any garden without yearly treatment. If you are not organic then treated wood will suffice but bear in mind that you do get what you pay for, so always examine the quality of the materials before buying.

Mr. Ron Jenkins from Coventry. Says that his Agapanthus plants have grown well for some years, but only has leaves and no flowers any suggestions?

There are some fairly simple remedies to this problem. These plants are natives of South Africa and they require a sunny and well drained position. If they are denied enough sunlight flower buds will not be produced by the plants. When plants are put into the ground, even from pots, they do suffer a shock and this can result in one of three things. Either they can grow away perfectly well as if nothing has happened or they can put on lots of leaf and no flower or they can sit there, not grow but flower away madly! What they need is something to knock them back onto the right track, so try applying high potash feed. A large congested clump will also give few if any flowers on most perennials, so if your clump is big and seems packed full of shoots, divide it in the autumn or spring and replace with lots of smaller clumps to give a similar effect.

Mrs. Dewar in Dunstable. Has a small garden and would like to grow one or two trees, can you suggest some please?

The Sorbus is one of our favourite small trees with several different varieties fitting the bill. All of them produce flowers in the spring followed by lovely clusters of pendulous fruits in the autumn. In addition to the fantastic autumn colour they do not cast deep shade which is a real asset in a small garden. Sorbus cashmiriana – large white fruits and only growing to 3m (10'), commixta – bright red fruits and growing to 10m (30') and vilmorinii – dark red fruits ripening to pink and then white and growing to about 5m (15') are on our 'must have' list. Cornus altenifolia 'Argentea' is a small tree, only getting to 6m (20') that is interesting all year round. Cotoneaster 'Cornubia' flowers in the spring and produces a plentiful crop of bright red berries. It is semi-evergreen and has a pendulous habit, achieving about 6m (20') in height.

Mrs. P. Day from Northamptonshire. Wants advice on types of winter flowering perennials to grow in an herbaceous border.

Not an easy question to answer as winter flowering perennials are few and far between. A classic winter and early spring flowering perennial is the Hellebore. To enjoy the flowers of orientalis varieties at their best remember to cut off all the old leaves just as the flower buds begin to open. Iris unguicularis flowers during the winter and it takes a hard frost very well. The strange and diminutive Hacquetia epipactis has a mound of tiny yellow flowers surrounded by a rosette of yellow-green bracts. All of these are fairly low growing but will give flower interest in your border when most herbaceous perennials are not even showing signs of life.

Cathryn Frost from Matlock. Would like to know what are the best apple varieties to grow for step-over areas? *I think Nick needs to explain a step-over area first!*

The rootstock is all important. As a 'step-over' tree is usually trained onto a wire 45cm (18") from the ground you do not want to use a variety on too vigorous a rootstock because this will be difficult to maintain at a low enough level. Some apple varieties do not perform well on a dwarfing rootstock, so look for a variety you like on a dwarfing rootstock such as M9 and that should do the job perfectly.

Mrs. Dorothy Redrup from Bracknell. Desperately needs to know how to get rid of vine weevils in her garden.

We find that the best method is to use nematodes as a natural predator. The newer nematodes are active at temperatures down to 5 degrees centigrade and can be applied from March onwards. These nematodes are microscopic and will only attack vine weevils, so all your other beneficial insects will be safe. Nematodes are very easy to apply, simply add them to a full watering can and water onto the affected areas or pots. If you have an attack in pots then clean the compost from the roots and dispose of it in the bin before washing the roots and repotting the plant. Being vigilant also helps because adult weevils can be spotted and squashed between finger and thumb before they get a chance to lay any eggs.

D. A. Doyle in Kettering. Wants to know how to keep whitefly off indoor plants.

Whitefly is definitely a persistent pest but it can be controlled. We use natural predators, such as Encarsia Formosa which is a parasitic wasp only attracted to the whitefly scales where it lays its eggs and kills the larvae before they emerge. Whitefly can be sprayed, if you prefer to use that method, with derris or a proprietary whitefly spray. If you decide to use a spray pick a still day and treat the plant outdoors. On less delicate plants a sharp squirt of water can dislodge a lot of flies and scales – do this outdoors to avoid a flooded carpet! Your best tool against pests and disease is vigilance. Get to the pest before it takes hold.

Ian McCurrach in Aberdeenshire. How can I eradicate black spot from my roses?

The most important point to bear in mind with regard to rose black spot is that it over winters on the leaves. Hygiene is your best form of attack. In the autumn pick up all the fallen leaves and compost them or bin or burn them and this will prevent the spore re-infecting the following year's roses. Bordeaux mixture is a spray that can be used if you are gardening organically. Proprietary products are available from garden centres but you must start spraying at regular intervals when the first leaves appear. Unfortunately this disease is fast becoming much more prevalent and harder to control. At Barnsdale we enjoy the beauty of the flowers and disregard the spotty foliage!

Part Two – Trees

For centuries trees have adorned the landscape of our countryside. As children we played in the woods and used the timber to make bows and arrows and other implements as well as 'camps' to play in. Little did we realise that some of those very trees have stood for centuries and borne silent witness to our history. When we plant a tree we are planting something for the future, something our children and grandchildren will admire and wonder at. It is worth bearing this thought in mind when you choose a tree for your garden, or it may simply be that you want a tree to enjoy for now and there is nothing wrong in that. For my own part I want my kids to admire a tree that I planted when I am long gone. On my regular visits to Barnsdale, I have been taken with the way the gardens change with the seasons. It's true that some people visit in December and mutter, "I thought there would be more plants in flower". I'm afraid that I simply cannot subscribe to this view as THERE'S ALWAYS SOMETHING TO SEE IF YOU REALLY LOOK. At Barnsdale the seasons have been catered for and some of the trees are really at their best when other plants and shrubs are taking a well earned rest. It's called planning.

Acer palmatum 'Beni-schichihenge', Acer griseum, Acer platanoides 'Crimson Sentry' and Acer palmatum 'Sango-kaku'

For me any Acer will do and they are quite adaptable. With beautifully coloured barks and leaves they really do deserve a special place in any garden. See what Nick has to say after you have admired these photographs of some of the Acers at Barnsdale.

Acer palmatum 'Beni-schichihenge'

Acer palmatum 'Sango-kaku'

Acer platanoides 'Crimson Sentry'

Nick Says: "Acer palmatum 'Beni-schichihenge' is the tree most visitors comment on during the spring, early summer and autumn. We have two growing in large pots near the Country Garden and this is one of the most spectacular varieties I have seen. It emerges in spring with the green and cream variegated leaves having a distinct and incredibly bright orange-pink flush, which gradually fades through the season leaving a green and cream variegation. We enhance the pink flush by being stingy on the feed and a little less flowing with the water in the early part of the season. You have to be careful as you don't want to under water to the point where the leaves are scorched. Although it will grow in sun or semi-shade, it is important to plant in an area where it is not affected by the cold spring winds as the leaf edges will turn brown.

Acer griseum is a contrast to my first choice as it is at its best from late autumn into early spring. When the leaves start to fall and the autumn flowering perennials begin to fade this tree edges itself towards the front of the border, until it gets to that time of year when you cannot fail to stop and admire it. We deliberately have it planted in an area where this is the case so that it can stand with nothing detracting from its beauty. The lovely orange-brown bark peels on both trunk and branches and, as it's a slowly spreading tree, it will fit into most gardens.

I thought hard before including Acer platanoides 'Crimson Sentry' because of its mildew problem but then I decided that this was a small price to pay for such a gorgeous tree. It stands erect and columnar, ultimately getting to 12m (40') and is covered with lovely large, crimson-purple, palmate leaves which produce warm, glowing winter colours. In most years mildew will affect the leaves, generally late in the season, and it's best to collect them up and burn or bin them.

I have included another Japanese Maple but I couldn't resist it as Acer palmatum 'Sango-kaku' (also known as 'Senkaki') must surely be on most people's tree list. It has the most spectacular orange-yellow leaves that turn soft yellow in autumn and then seems to go through a metamorphosis to become a Cornus, giving stunning bright red shoots through the winter."

Amelanchier lamarckii

A small tree but sometimes size doesn't matter and in the case of this variety the sentiment is true! It has white haired young shoots but they soon lose that hair. (Ring any bells, Nick?)

Nick Says: "I'll have you know that my head has always been evergreen with no signs of it becoming deciduous. If it's spring colour you want with a bit extra in the autumn then this is the tree for you. It is a small and upright tree that is absolutely covered with pendant racemes of long white flowers in mid-spring followed

by purple-black fruit. The young leaves emerge bronze-tinted and mature to dark green. There is then a very minor lull before the leaves begin to turn in the autumn producing the most magnificent shades of orange and red that are as warming on those chilly autumn mornings as a raging log fire!"

Arbutus menziesii

There are some fourteen species of these evergreen trees or shrubs with oval, toothed leaves and white flowers.

Sue Says: "The flowers of this variety are produced freely in erect panicles during early summer and are followed by spherical orange-red fruit. I grow it because of the interest given by the peeling red-brown bark that comes away leaving the perfectly smooth new bark, a bit like a snake shedding its old skin. I have had to plant it in a sunny, sheltered part of the garden as in Rutland it might suffer during the winter in more exposed parts."

Betula utilis jacquemontii and Betula papyrifera

There are about sixty species in this genus of deciduous trees and shrubs. Birches have wonderful leaves and barks that will adorn any garden. I particularly enjoy visiting Barnsdale in winter when these wonderful trees stand like sculptures as a testament to the theory that 'there is always something to see in a garden'.

Nick Says: "We are particularly fond of Betula utilis jacquemontii at Barnsdale and as John has already pointed out it is primarily for their winter beauty, although don't discount them as unimportant in the summer. We have found that multi-stemmed birch are a fantastic investment, as you get much more stem for your money and therefore much more impact in your garden. Our secret to beautiful white stems in the winter is firstly to be patient and wait for the whiteness to intensify as the tree matures and secondly, to dash out with a stiff brush and bowl of soapy water in the dead of night when none of the neighbours are watching to scrub stems! This needs to be done every couple of years as the stems attract algae and lichens, which dull that beautiful winter display.

Betula papyrifera has similar qualities, the difference being that when the white older bark peels it reveals the newer pale orange-brown bark beneath, giving an excellent colour variation."

Betula papyrifera

Betula utilis jacquemontii

Carpinus betulus

Otherwise known as the common Hornbeam, which is common only because they are plentiful and doesn't mean you shouldn't have one! The mid green leaves of summer turn yellow to orange in autumn.

Sue Says: "We have used this tree in the Country Paradise Garden and trained several into the arbour where there is a home built log seat. I love to sit in it in the spring when all the yellow male catkins are hanging just above my head. The female catkins will produce hanging green fruit later in the year. If left it will reach 25m (80') but we trim ours with hedge cutters once a year."

Cercidiphyllum japonicum

The shoots bear opposite, sometimes alternate, ovate midgreen leaves which emerge bronze-tinted.

Nick Says: "This was my father's favourite tree and in all the books that I have seen it listed, they state that it prefers a neutral to acid soil – however, we have two growing perfectly happily in a soil that has a pH of 8.3. Apart from the lovely spring leaf colour and the gorgeous butter-yellow of the falling leaves in autumn we grow this tree for the sumptuous sweet toffee smell produced as the leaves begin to turn colour in the late summer. Visitors to the gardens will spend hours looking for the flower producing this wonderful smell only to be shocked when they discover it is actually the leaves of a tree! Be warned, your waistline will expand if you have this tree in your garden after the inevitable regular trips to the sweet shop for bags of toffee!"

Cornus controversa 'Variegata' and Cornus 'Eddie's White Wonder'

'Dogwoods' are often grown for their 'showy' bracts, fruit and colourful autumn leaves. They are particularly good in woodland gardens and some have smashing coloured winter shoots. They have become popular alongside main roads and on roundabouts so keep your eyes open.

Sue Says: "Both the varieties I have chosen are slightly different and give interest above and beyond that of most dogwoods. Cornus controversa 'Variegata' is probably my favourite tree with its branches arranged in tiers and covered with white margined, green leaves. In fact, every time I look at it, it reminds me of a large wedding cake. It also blooms with the small white flowers appearing during early summer and followed by small blue-black fruit. In the autumn the leaves take on reddish tinges before they fall to expose a gorgeous framework that will provide interest throughout the winter. As temperatures drop, the twigs will turn a much more vibrant reddish-purple to enhance the tree's tiered structure.

Cornus 'Eddie's White Wonder' is another small tree, only reaching 6m (20') but you don't have to be big to be beautiful. In late spring it produces purplish-green flowers but these are not that significant only being 1cm (half inch) across. It is the five to six large white bracts that surround these small flowers that give this tree amazing spring interest. Mind you, it does not end there as in the autumn the mid-green leaves will take on wonderful orange, red and purple tones before falling."

Cornus controversa 'Variegata'

Corylus colurna

Hazels have wonderful catkins and beautiful foliage. This particular variety produces edible nuts enclosed in fringed husks in autumn.

Nick Says: "Known as the 'Turkish Hazel', this 20m (70') tree has a conical habit producing masses of pendant, yellow catkins in winter and edible nuts in autumn. I like it not only for what the tree yields but also because it has a nice form throughout the year, lovely yellow leaves in autumn and interesting bark."

Crataegus persimilis 'Prunifolia'

You may find that powdery mildew can be a problem. No, let me write that again! *You* won't find powdery mildew a problem but the plants might. This particular variety has splendid deep green leaves, which turn orange and red in autumn.

Nick Says: "We have never had a problem with mildew and neither have any of these trees in our garden. I'm a sucker for good value and this tree is certainly that. In early summer there is a plentiful show of white flowers held in flat corymbs amongst the shiny, dark green leaves. These are then followed by hanging bunches of spherical, bright red fruit that last well after the leaves have fallen and until the birds have had their fill. A spectacular 'Hawthorn' for any garden, as it will slowly reach about 8m (25'), producing a lovely rounded head in the process."

Eucalyptus pauciflora niphophila

Many European specimens grow to a height of 50m (160') so choose your variety and planting position carefully. They are sensitive to the cold but if you can get most varieties through their first winter they should be hardy enough to survive the rest. More tender varieties are fine in milder areas of the country.

Sue Says: "I love the sun and every time I look at this tree all I do is imagine hot, sunny Australian summers, particularly on damp, cold Rutland days. Most varieties are grown for their juvenile leaves but this one has a much more interesting bark that has a grey and white skinned snake feel about it. Although you can grow it as a large, single stemmed tree I find that to get the best out of it, it needs to be grown as a multi-stem. This means taking out the growing tip at an early age and allowing about 4 to 6 stems to be produced which will not only intensify the bark effect but also reduce its height and therefore make it a much more manageable tree. Nobody has been seen to walk straight past our multi-stemmed Eucalyptus without stopping and looking it up and down."

Euonymus planipes

An upright deciduous tree that produces wonderful autumnal coloured leaves and red fruit.

Nick Says: "As with most of the fruiting Euonymus, the pink-red fruit open out like an umbrella in the autumn to reveal the bright orange seeds. However, I like to have this plant in the garden for its autumn leaf effects because when you have a fully grown specimen of 3m (10') and you come across it in your garden during October, it's just like a pyromaniac got there fractionally before you and your instant reaction is to chuck a bucket of water over it to extinguish the flames!"

Ginko biloba

Known as the Maidenhair tree, it has furrowed dull grey bark and flat, fan shaped leaves.

Sue Says: "This is the oldest known variety of conifer although it is often mistaken for an ornamental tree. The unusual, flat fan-shaped green leaves are lobed at the tips and turn a wonderful shade of yellow in the autumn before they fall to the ground. This slow-growing tree will ultimately reach 30m (100') although I won't be here to see it. I do hope that ours produces fruit because I would like to try the edible nuts if I can bear to go past the rather unpleasantly smelling flesh of the fruit. Various parts of this tree have been used for centuries to treat a wide range of illnesses including stomach problems and breathing difficulties as well as enhancing sexual energy and improving your short term memory, although I can't quite remember which parts do what!"

Ilex x altaclerensis 'Lawsoniana'

There are over four hundred species of Holly and Kew Gardens have a wonderful display. Nick has chosen this female version (always one for the ladies, Nick?).

Nick Says: For a smaller garden this is an excellent choice as it has interesting leaves as well as berries, if there is a male near by. The real bonus for this variety is that it produces the most wonderful dark green leaves that are irregularly splashed with gold and

lighter green and in late summer, to cap it all off, it could be covered with an abundance of red berries. Although most hollies can be kept under control by regular clipping, such as taking bits for flower arranging or just cutting off shoots that are growing too vigorously during summer, this variety only grows to 6m (20').

Laburnum x waterii 'Vossii'

Don't eat any part of this tree as it's dangerous, so if you have young children it's best to avoid it. This particular variety however does have wonderful golden yellow flowers.

Sue Says: "We have this growing over a pergola just by the rose garden and accompanied by Clematis, Roses, Wisteria and Akebia. There can be nothing more heartening to the soul than walking through the pergola with the long, pendant racemes of pea-like, golden-yellow flowers falling in a shower of sunshine above your head. Although the seeds are poisonous this shouldn't put you off, you can easily remove the seed-pods before they ripen. It's a small price to pay for such a remarkable tree."

Liquidamber styraciflua

With its Maple-like leaves this plant is another 'special' for the autumn. The young shoots often have 'corky' like wings on young shoots.

Nick Says: "I absolutely love the autumn and this tree would be in any garden that I owned simply because of its spectacular autumnal display. The combination of orange, red and purple colours on the large palmate leaves of a fully mature specimen of 25m (80') is enough to stop anybody in their tracks and to leave them standing in awe."

Liriodendron tulipifera 'Aureomarginatum'

Very stately with odd shaped leaves which colour in autumn. The single flowers are cup shaped and do not look much until you get up close but they make great specimen trees.

Liriodendron tulipifera

Sue Says: "This is the more unusual form which gives extra interest through the summer months. It produces fantastic pale green, tulip-like flowers that have a distinct orange band around the base in midsummer as well as large dark green leaves. This variety has a lovely golden-yellow margin to the leaves. It will grow up to 20m (70') high over quite a long period and it is possible to grow it in either sun or semi-shade in a neutral to acid soil."

Magnolia grandiflora and Magnolia x soulangeana

I've never been too keen on Magnolias but I was impressed when I saw the specimen at Barnsdale. With its large, cup shaped white flowers that can grow to as much as ten inches across, it really is a beauty.

Nick Says: "Magnolia grandiflora is, in my view, the best wall shrub around, producing massive creamy-white flowers that have the most amazing lemon scent, among glossy, evergreen leaves in late summer and autumn. Floating in a bowl of water, the flowers will spread scent around the whole house. Mind you it's not for this reason that it will always have a very special place in my heart. No, it is because it made me look a fool many years ago. It was while I was working at a large wholesale nursery in Norfolk that I took five cuttings from a plant growing on the wall of a local manor house. Remarkably, as I had no propagation system except for a pot, compost and a plastic bag, all five rooted and I gave them away to friends, colleagues and my dad – BIG MISTAKE! He planted his in an open border just opposite where he would eventually site his pond and stream. "It will never grow there," I said, "because it is a wall shrub and in the midlands, needs the protection of a south or west facing wall." "I think it will be fine just where it is" came the curt reply. Twenty years on it is thriving and flowering better than ever. I was made to swallow my pride many times.

Magnolia x soulangeana, although fairly common in gardens, is a stately plant that each spring produces a cascade of goblet-shaped flowers. Unless buying a named hybrid, the species is variable with flowers ranging from deep rose-pink right through to white. For best results plant in a neutral to acid soil."

Magnolia x soulangeana

Malus 'Evereste'

There are about thirty five species of Malus (often called crab apples). This particular tree has dark green leaves and produces white flowers in late spring.

Sue Says: "This is a fantastic tree that will not only pollinate dessert and cooking apples in your garden but also give masses of interest during spring and autumn. In spring the tree produces so many white flowers from reddish buds that you cannot see the leaves. These are followed in late summer and autumn by just as many orange-yellow fruits that can be made into preserves or left

for the birds to enjoy. A difficult variety to put a height on as it depends on which rootstock it is grafted onto but can easily be kept under control by regular pruning."

Metasequoia glyptostroboides

I have always throught that a redwood is too large for any garden, so tell me more, Nick.

Nick Says: "A variety of redwood, but not the giant kind, although this tree does ultimately reach between 20-40m (70-140') high. That said, we have one growing in the gardens in a drier spot and this does seem to curtail the growth rate. It is one of those unusual conifers which lose their leaves in the autumn, but don't let this put you off as it is a fascinating tree. The gnarled and ridged trunk is worthy of a place in the garden on its own merits but added to that are soft, bright green leaves that make up the perfect cone-shaped tree. An added quirk and one to stun your friends with is that the buds are not produced in the leaf axils as with virtually every other plant or tree variety but they appear below the leaf stalk, making this tree one of the easiest to identify!"

Picea pungens 'Koster'

Spruce is, without doubt, a hardy tree and therefore a 'tree for all seasons'. I suspect that Sue has chosen this particular variety because of its beautiful silvery blue foliage.

Sue Says: "I must admit that I am not the biggest fan of conifers but this one will get my vote every time. It always looks so perfect in shape almost as if the branches have been immaculately placed so that each has its own space in which to shine. It's not a small conifer, ultimately reaching 15m (50'), but will take its time getting there and in that time you'll enjoy the sparkling needles through every week of every year."

Prunus x subhirtella 'Autumnalis'

We are back to my old dad again with Prunus! Dad purchased a Prunus pissardii when he won the football pools back in the year dot. He bought a bicycle and a pen as well! I have always planted Prunus in every garden I have owned ever since that day.

Nick Says: "As you have probably guessed by now I am a great fan of autumn colour, but I do like to see flowers in the garden during winter as they never fail to lift my spirits. This small tree reaching only 8m (25') will flower intermittently during mild spells from autumn right through winter and into spring, bearing double, pink-tinged white flowers. This is one of the more subtle and less garish of the flowering cherries."

Prunus padus

Sue Says: "This is a fairly uninteresting tree for most of the year but when it bursts into life during late spring it does so with a vengeance. An abundance of racemes of white flowers up to 15cm (7") long resemble those of a Buddleia flower cone but have the added bonus of a quite powerful fragrance, which often surprises many of our visitors who have never before come across this tree. It will need space to develop as ultimately it will grow to about 15m (50') high with a 10m (35') spread."

Prunus scrrula

They make very good specimen trees and some work particularly well in smaller gardens.

Nick Says: "Without wanting to sound too perverted, this is unquestionably our most fondled tree in the whole garden! It does flower although you would be doing extremely well to spot the small white flowers when they appear in April, and it does produce some reasonable leaf colours in autumn, but not spectacular. Not sounding too good for an ornamental cherry is it? That is until you see the quite spectacular shiny, almost polished red-brown, mahogany-like bark that just makes you want to rub it up and down. Honestly, you really can't help yourself! The bark on the stem and branches peels, which adds to its overall beauty and gives it that extra special place in any garden, but it must be planted where you can touch it otherwise you'll find yourself trampling through borders to reach it. I haven't come across a more tactile tree or one that looks so spectacular 365 days a year."

Prunus 'Shirotae'

Sue Says: "You will also find this tree listed as Prunus 'Mount Fuji' but they are both one and the same. A must if you have the space, not because it reaches any great height but because the top spreads to 8m (25') wide. You may regard this as a problem but just imagine it covered with single and semi-double cup-shaped fragrant white flowers during spring and that problem will gently drift away. In the autumn it also produces lovely leaf tones in orange and red. We have a tree in the garden that I have not seen elsewhere, which has Prunus 'Shirotae' grafted onto a stem of Prunus serrula - now that's a tree that has it all!"

Quercus ilex

The Holm Oak is an evergreen with dark grey bark and dark green leaves, a real stunner all year round, so I'll let Sue tell you more.

Sue Says: "I like the idea of an evergreen Oak. The leaves resemble those of a Holly, hence the Ilex part of the name. It produces the classically rounded head you would expect from an Oak and even produces rounded acorns. Best of all, for those of you who have enough leaves to rake up in the autumn, it looks good all year round. It will reach a height of 25m (80') and a spread of 20m (70') but only in your great, great, great, great, great grand-children's lifetime, if you're lucky."

Sorbus cashmiriana

There are several species and varieties within the genus Sorbus and they can differ both in size and in the colour of their foliage. When planted as a single specimen tree, a Sorbus provides a pleasant shady spot.

Sue Says: "This variety of Mountain Ash will fit into any garden as it only reaches 3m (10') but it packs a lot into a small tree. In spring it produces an abundance of small pinkish-white flowers in flattened corymbs that are followed in late summer by hanging bunches of large white berries. For longevity on the tree, the white berries are one of the last that the birds will eat, but once they have ploughed through the red, pink and yellow berries the white ones are the equivalent of coffee and a mint."

Sorbus thibetica 'John Mitchell'

Nick Says: "Whenever I talk to people about Sorbus they immediately think of masses of white flowers in the spring followed by great clusters of berries in the autumn. Not me, I think of John Mitchell, strange I know, but those of you who know the tree will understand my thinking. Don't get me wrong, I like the others and we have many different varieties planted around the gardens that feed the birds very well through the autumn and into the winter,

but this tree is grown for its quite spectacular leaves. The massive leaves are green above and white tomentose beneath, so that when there is a breeze it gives a quite spectacular effect. It grows into a medium-sized tree about 20m high with a rounded head and does bear fruit, although they are large, fairly uninteresting and brown. The only drawback we have found with it is that it holds onto those enormous leaves longer than most trees, which can be a problem when we get strong autumn winds."

Barnsdale's Own Gardeners' Question Time - Part 2

Some more Gardeners' Questions answered by Nick and Sue.

Catherine Wilson from Whissendine. Thinks that she might be asking the impossible! She wants to know if you can recommend a shrub to suit the heavy clay environment at Whissendine? She wants something that has good foliage in winter, an attractive flower and smells good. Price would not be important if all of these criteria were met!

There is not sufficient space here to list them all and your best bet is to come and see what spectacular shrubs we have at Barnsdale on the same heavy clay. What about Mahonia? It is an underrated shrub, with lovely autumn leaf tints, excellent colour in new spring growth and scented yellow flowers in winter/spring. It also grows almost anywhere. Viburnum x burkwoodii is a semi-evergreen shrub that produces lovely scented white flowers in winter/spring and glossy green leaves. In a sheltered part of the garden it should be possible to grow one of the Choisyas which have interesting, evergreen leaves and scented white flowers. You might also get away with Cytisus battandieri against a warm wall, provided you improve the soil with compost and coarse grit. It has lovely pineapple-scented, yellow flowers and soft, silver-grey leaves.

Jenny Hurley from Norwich. Asks how do you get rid of ground elder from your garden?

If you are not an organic gardener the best method is to apply herbicide containing glyphosate and keep applying it until you have totally eradicated the problem. Use a sprayer over a large area that contains no plants, but if it has run riot through part of a border then you can apply the herbicide directly to the leaves using a paint brush. Remember to wear the appropriate protective clothing when dealing with any herbicide or pesticide. If you are organic the method is less straight forward and really boils down to continual pulling. This will weaken the plant and it will eventually die out. Covering the area with black polythene may also help.

Lynne Sutton-How in Kent. How tall does Laburnum grow? At the moment we have ours in a large pot.

Most Laburnums grow to about 8m (25') high so your pot will need to be very large! Regular pruning after flowering will keep it down to a manageable size. We have a Laburnum x watereri 'Vossii' over part of a pergola and with annual pruning it is kept very nicely under control.

Stanley Davies from Wigston. What treatment is best to get rid of excessive moss on a lawn that, in wet conditions, gets quite boggy?

The remedy is to improve the drainage in your lawn. If you get the grass growing strongly this will prevent moss. In the spring rake out the moss either with a spring tined rake or you could hire a scarifier. Then use a fork to make regular, deep holes across the lawn. These holes should be filled with sharp sand which will begin to improve the drainage of your grass. Then you need to give your lawn a feed to boost it into growth so that it can compete with any returning moss. This should be done each year until the lawn has improved.

Robert Kilford in Lincoln. Wants you to recommend some small shrubs for a rockery/pond surround.

We like Salix 'Mark Postill' particularly near water as the willows tend to be waterside natives. It will only get to between 30-60cm (12"-24") in height. For a rockery we would always have a Helianthemum because they flower all summer and only reach 20-30cm (8"-12") in height. Berberis atropurpurea 'Nana' is a compact little shrub whilst Cornus stolonifera 'Kelseyi', though not so well known, has delightful red tipped, yellow-green winter stems only 60cm (24") tall.

Richard Turpin from Northampton. Asks a simple and straightforward question, he wants to know how to get rid of rust on hollyhocks.

You can't! It is just one of those diseases that seem to be resistant to virtually every fungicide so, in a bad year, you will get it I'm afraid.

John Dunkley in Nether Heyford. Asks if pruning Bramley apples will affect the yield and will they fruit on old wood.

Apples will fruit on wood that is between 1 and 3 years old. It is the pruning method that is all important. Bramley is a tip bearer so needs to be lightly pruned in the winter, with the tips being cut back just far enough and without removing too many fruit buds. Remove any unproductive, overcrowded, crossing or diseased branches. Any side shoots less than 30cm long should be left. Because Bramley is a vigorous tree it should always be grown on a dwarfing rootstock to control the size.

Mary Ellis from near Taunton, Devon. Would like to know the best way to stop birds from eating grass seed.

We find that our cat usually does the trick, although he also tends to dig holes right in the middle of our nicely leveled and seeded ground. Our method is to over seed slightly and in this way, when the birds do feed, they fly away with full stomachs and leave us with seed to spare. It is also a good idea to sow your seed when a mild but wet period is forecast so that the seed germinates quickly and gets going before the birds get to it.

Mrs. S. Whiteman in Windsor. Says that she has a 'Geoff Hamilton' Penstemon plant and would like to know how hard it needs to be cut back and should this be done in winter or spring?

This fantastic plant benefits, as do most hybrid Penstemon, from being cut back hard around mid to late April. At that time of year there will be a mass of new shoots forming at the base of the plant, which is where you should cut back to. This will help the plant to live longer and keep it flowering beautifully.

Mrs. Mary Nourish from Uppingham, Rutland. Has an area of garden dominated by two very large sycamore trees, the ground underneath is dry and covered with ivy. She grows snowdrops in the spring and wants you to suggest some plants for summer colour and interest.

Planting under trees is always difficult but planting under large trees with dry soil is just about the worst position! What you need to look at is the range of plants that will normally take over a garden which has a perfect soil. These plants will have the vigour to survive in difficult conditions. Vinca is the ideal example, it will flower in spring and often again in late summer, with some varieties also having variegated foliage to add more interest. Quite a few varieties of Geranium will grow and flower during the summer. Tellima grandiflora 'Rubra Group' is a lovely plant with reddish leaves all year and greenish-yellow flowers. Euphorbia should also do well, amygdaloides 'Robbiae' with its spring flower display and interesting leaves or cyparissias 'Fens Ruby', again with lovely spring flowers and narrow purple-red leaves.

Mrs. Stephen in Aberdeenshire. Wants to know why her Hydrangea never flowers, should it be cut back at any special time of year?

Pruning Hydrangeas is vitally important because most will flower on wood made the previous year, if you prune all over in the autumn or spring you will be removing the flowering shoots. For all macrophylla types, which are the most commonly available, prune back the shoots that have just flowered to a healthy set of buds and leave everything else. Pruning in this manner should be carried out in this way each year.

Mrs. Mary Manley from Bedfordshire. When and how do you prune Garrya? I'm training it against a trellis. It is about 6 years old, was moved about 3 years ago and has not produced tassels.

To keep a Garrya under control and nicely trained all pruning should be carried out in late spring, after flowering. It's difficult to judge exactly if your plant is not flowering! It may have been the shock of moving it that has caused it not to produce tassels yet, or it may be that you do not have the right variety. The best variety that produces the longest tassels is Garrya elliptica 'James Roof'. You could also try feeding your plant with a high potash feed through the growing season this will encourage it to flower the following winter.

Mrs. M. Davies in Wigston, Leicestershire. Wants to know how to stop a blackish mould on a white Jasmine shrub. The mould is on the leaves and the stems otherwise the plant is alive but has not flowered this year.

It sounds like you have sooty mould, which is a harmless mould that grows on the secretions made by pests such as whiteflies and mealy bugs. If your plant is outside then spraying is the answer. Use an appropriate organic or inorganic pesticide. If your plant is indoors you should consider using natural predators.

Dave Shaw from Sandhurst, Berkshire. Wants to know how long he should wait before he can use the leaves from his leaf compost store.

This very much depends on which leaves you are composting and how it is done. It will usually take between 2-3 years for them to rot down to a usable state but you can speed the process up by using a closed bin or collecting the leaves with a lawnmower so that they get partially shredded and therefore rot quicker.

Charles Hughes in Woodhall Spa, Lincolnshire. Makes a good point. We can plant for drought conditions but how can we prepare soil for long term drought? *Organically of course.*

Adding organic matter to the soil is an excellent way to conserve moisture that can be drawn on by plant roots. Farm yard manure, garden compost, green compost, etc will all do the trick. Covering the soil with a 5-7cm (2"-3") of mulch will help to stop evaporation from the soil surface. Bark and recycled glass is also good. At Barnsdale we also use a leaky pipe attached to a water butt and laid near to plant roots. The pipe is made from recycled rubber and it works under very low pressure so the water can come straight off the water butt and gravity will do the rest.

Jean Mason in Burton on Trent. Asks how she can prevent grubs on plums?

It sounds very much as if your plants are suffering from plum sawfly. They pupate in the soil so regular hoeing will expose the pupae to the birds and give them a free and easy lunch. If this fails then an insecticide spray after the petals have fallen should do the trick. We would use derris.

Alan Walker from Swadlincote. Wonders why rhubarb flowers and is it correct to cut the flowers as they develop.

Rhubarb is really a vegetable and we eat the stems and not the fruit, it is also perennial. If it is grown as an ornamental plant it is classed as 'having lovely leaves and a robust flower spike'. We grow it for the usefulness of the stems and so our preference is that it should not flower and waste energy. If your plant starts to send up a flower spike cut it off, chop it up, put it onto the compost heap and then enjoy the abundance of stems that follow in a good old fashioned crumble!

Rosemary Dunkley in Nether Heyford. Has a tree Peony and wants to know about pruning after flowering?

These large shrubs require minimal pruning and what needs to be pruned is generally best cut out in late winter or early spring. Simply remove crossing, dead or wayward shoots and cut back to a point at which they add to the balanced framework of your shrub.

Mr. K. Sawford in Kettering. Wants to know how and when to prune Hebes. They maintain their shape perfectly but get progressively too large for their space.

As these are temperate climate plants it is not wise to prune before early spring in case we get a very hard winter. It is very much a case of light trimming all over during spring to keep the balanced look of your plant. If it has wildly grown out of its space then they will grow back, most of the time, from a very hard prune. This involves cutting back to about 10-15cm (4"-6") from the ground, crossing everything and hoping for the best! Most do shoot but it really is a last resort.

Shirley Webb in Hillmorton, Warwickshire. Wants to know which is your favourite part of Barnsdale and why.

Nick says: It has to be the Ornamental Kitchen Garden because it has a bit of everything growing in it along with great structural interest from trees and shrubs as well as from the diagonal, straight and bendy paths.

Sue says: The Japanese Garden, not just because I designed it, but also because it is so different from the other gardens at Barnsdale and because of the very positive responses we keep getting from the people who see it.

Vera Knapton from Hadleigh, Essex. Asks if there is any product on the market that would restrict the outward growth of Bamboo roots.

The obvious answer that springs to my mind is a spade! If you have space for one of the more vigorous, spreading varieties then all well and good, but if you don't, the answer is that you are much better off with a clump-forming variety that does not run. Clump-formers such as Fargesia nitida, will gradually produce a lovely, very easily manageable clump that will require dividing from time to time but will not need to be contained.

Madeleine Jones lives near Benfleet. She would like to know if it is possible to grow mistletoe from seed in a small garden.

Yes, it certainly is. The best time to propagate it is any time from March to April when the seed is fully ripe. If you are collecting the seed yourself do try to get it from Mistletoe growing on a similar type of tree to the one you have in your garden, but if this is not possible it should still germinate. Apple trees make excellent host plants. Make a small insertion into a reasonably sized branch that gets a good amount of sunlight and slip the seed just under the bark. It needs to be covered with something breathable to prevent the birds getting to it. Just bear in mind that it does not germinate particularly well and that you need both male and female plants for the female to berry. Therefore you will need to carry out this procedure with several seeds. Good luck and a Merry Christmas!

Eileen Southwell from Hadleigh. Asks when she should prune Lonicera fragrantissima?

This shrub flowers during winter and early spring and it does so on the growth it produced during the previous summer. Therefore any pruning should be carried out after flowering in the spring.

Mary Hawthorne from Essex. Wants to know where she can get Angels Fishing Rod and how should she look after it?

The plant you are looking for is a Dierama and they are available from a lot of nurseries around the country, including Barnsdale. They are mostly seen with the flowers hanging out over water giving the impression that they like a heavy, wet soil. This is not the case as their ideal position is in full sun growing in a free draining soil but planting by the edge of a pond would be fine as long as it isn't in the bog area.

Liz Humphrey is from Helmdon. She has a double white Arabis and would like to know when and how is the best way to propagate it?

Once your plant has finished flowering it will begin to grow away and it is the soft tips that can be taken as 3-5cm (1"-2") cuttings. They are relatively easy to propagate and can be rooted into a cuttings compost in a greenhouse or under a cold frame.

Part Three – Vegetables, Herbs and Fruit

This is the section where both Sue and Nick come into their own – Nick grows them and Sue cooks them! That's OK with me because I can't really imagine eating anything that Nick has cooked. The fruit and vegetable areas at Barnsdale are a constant source of wonder to me. In my own garden I don't have the space to grow much in the way of items 'for the table' but it's still possible for me to enjoy the fruits of my labour in a small way, thanks to the advice of Nick and Sue. As for herbs, well it can be so easy to integrate these plants into even the smallest garden and what a joy they can be. It's great to pick them fresh to be used in cooking but don't just leave it there as they can be enjoyed in the garden as plants in their own right, even if you are the worst chef in the world. So whether you have plenty of room or a limited space to grow fruit and vegetables, read on and Nick will give you some ideas.

Vegetables

Asparagus 'Cito'

This can be an expensive vegetable to buy, therefore it is a 'must' to grow. Contrary to common belief asparagus is quite simple to cultivate and will produce an excellent yield of large, straight spears each year. If your soil is very sandy and extremely well drained you can grow plants directly in the soil on ridges. However if, like us, you are not that lucky then you should grow your plants in a raised bed where you can give them the sharp drainage they require. If you are growing from a one-year-old crown then lightly pick the spears in the first year to encourage the crowns to increase in size, so that from the second year you can crop as much as you like until mid June. They should then be left to produce lovely, feathery green fronds that will grow 120-150cm (4'-5') high.

Broad Bean 'Aquadulce Claudia' and 'Crimson Flowered'

Where would we be without broad beans? We grow them at Barnsdale not simply to produce food for the table but also as a green manure to make food for the soil. The variety 'Aquadulce Claudia' is the earliest cropper which can be sown outside from late October. We cover ours with a cloche just to give it that extra protection if we get a hard winter and then follow that early sowing with another outside in February. The 'Crimson Flowered' broad bean is a Heritage Seed Variety available from an organic gardening catalogue. We start our crop in the greenhouse in pots during January and then plant them out under cloches in February. In my opinion, a vegetable plot would be a beautiful place even without the vegetables, and the crimson flowers on this variety will certainly add enormously to the look of any garden. At the end of October we use the broad bean seeds we have left over as a green manure on any spare piece of ground available on the vegetable plot.

Broad Bean 'Crimson Flowered'

French Bean 'Borlotto Firetongue', 'Purple Queen' and 'Cobra'

Having a French mother, these were inevitably going to be in the book as I was brought up on tons of French beans cooked with garlic. Having said that, the first variety that I have chosen is 'Borlotto Firetongue' and Italian (sorry, Mum), which is a dwarf type. We grow it not only because it tastes good when fresh or as haricot beans which will last for months in airtight jars, but also because of the fantastic colour of the pods. Dwarf French bean 'Purple Queen' is another we grow for the addition of colour to the vegetable plot and because the stringless pods also have a delicious flavour. The only disappointment with this variety is that the pods turn green as they are being cooked. Another invaluable French bean for us is the climbing variety 'Cobra' because it not only produces a crop of long, stringless pods which, if picked regularly, will keep producing until the autumn, but it is also possible to squeeze it into situations where you would not normally grow a vegetable. We have them growing up our pergolas in the Ornamental Kitchen Garden and the obelisks in the Parterre amongst the ornamental plants. It sometimes happens that a visitor asks us "what variety of rose has produced pods like that" and we don't have the heart to tell them that it is a vegetable!

French Bean 'Borlotto Firetongue'　　　　　　*French Bean 'Purple Queen'*

Runner Bean 'Painted Lady'

This well known variety is usually on most gardeners' seed order list and rightly so. It's easy to grow and produces an excellent show of bi-coloured red and white flowers and enough beans to keep even the largest family contented. We always grow our runners over a trench that has been filled with organic matter so that the plants have a continuous supply of water at their roots. This guarantees an excellent crop of beans year on year.

Beetroot 'Boltardy', 'Choggia Pink' and 'Pronto'

This is one of my favourites. I could quite easily keep eating beetroot until I turned into one. If you sow in succession this is a vegetable that should be available all year round, but you also need to adopt good storage practices. The variety 'Boltardy' is the most well known and reliably produces an excellent crop of rounded roots that, as the name suggests, are resistant to bolting. We sow it right through the season but find that it is the best variety for early sowing, particularly when multi-sown in modules in December for planting out under cloches. 'Choggia Pink' is a variety that doesn't show its true colours until served at the table, quite literally. It looks great when it is growing because it has a pinky-orange skin which contrasts nicely with the plum-purple of the other varieties, but wait! Because it's not until you cut horizontally through the flesh that you encounter the wonderful interior display. The white flesh is broken by solid rings of rose or red and the beauty is that it stays like that even after cooking. The last variety is essential for us because we do grow quite a lot of our vegetables on raised 120cm (4') beds and the baby veg really come into their own on that system. The variety 'Pronto' that has been bred to be picked when it is still small, about ping-pong ball size, so is suited to not only deep beds but multiple sowing in modules. 'Boltardy' can also be picked when small but 'Pronto', when left too long, will not produce a tasty large root.

Beetroot 'Boltardy'

Beetroot 'Pronto'

Beetroot 'Choggia Pink'

Brussels Sprout 'Red Delicious', 'Cumulus' and 'Montgomery'

I am a traditionalist and so for me Christmas is not Christmas without a large serving of Brussels sprouts. If you have a penchant for everything red at Yuletide then the variety 'Red Delicious' really comes into its own. The flavour is excellent and the plants produce full stems of good size sprouts. It was undoubtedly devastating to us 'sprouters' when it was announced that seed of the variety 'Peer Gynt' would no longer be available because we loved it so much, but fear not because we have discovered 'Cumulus' which is a most satisfactory replacement. It produces an excellent crop on long stems, with the sprouts capable of remaining on the stems for a long time without 'blowing'. Both of these varieties will produce sprouts for Christmas but I like to extend the sprout season by growing 'Montgomery', which gives excellent quality sprouts until at least the end of January.

Brussels Sprout 'Red Delicious'

Brussels Sprout 'Montgomery'

Brussels Sprout 'Cumulus'

Cabbage 'Golden Acre Primo', 'Red Drumhead', 'January King' and 'Greyhound'

For all cabbage lovers the good news is that we can be picking varieties of cabbage every week of the year. 'Golden Acre Primo' is a very versatile variety that produces a crop earlier than other summer maturing varieties and can be harvested from early July to November. 'Red Drumhead' is also a summer maturing variety that comes later than 'Golden Acre Primo' and will give additional colour to meals. Whilst the variety 'January King' will start to mature from December and sit well through the winter to be picked when required as well as filling the spring gap, we like 'Greyhound' with its pointed heads that not only look good in the vegetable plot but also have an excellent flavour. We find that sowing all varieties in seed trays works well for the early crops, whilst the main crop plants do better when raised in a seed bed and then planted out into their final positions from there. In our crop rotation we always follow our nitrogen fixing peas and beans with the brassicas because of the goodness which is already in the soil, and we then fertilise well with pelleted chicken manure prior to planting. Cabbages are an excellent source of vitamin A and C.

Cabbage 'January King'

Carrot 'Ideal', 'Early Nantes 5', 'Maestro' and 'Purple Haze'

With our heavy, stony soil at Barnsdale we have always struggled to get a decent crop of carrots, with Sue spending most of her time peeling an average of three legs per carrot! However, things are on the turn. After years of adding our own compost, well rotted farmyard manure and sand to the soil we are now starting to reap the rewards and are finally harvesting straight, single root carrots, much to Sue's delight. Carrot 'Ideal' has always been a 'good doer' for us as it is a baby vegetable and is quick to mature, has an excellent flavour raw or cooked and only has a short root and this is important on heavy soil. These days we also use it on our raised beds as well as in an early crop of multi-sown module raised carrots. The big problem with it is that hardly any reach the table as they are absolutely beautiful pulled fresh from the ground and eaten immediately. Well, that's my secret out because up until now I have always been able to get away with blaming the lack of crop on carrot root fly! As the name suggests, 'Early Nantes 5' is an excellent early variety that we raise under cloches and fleece, but we also continue it through the growing season with a succession of sowings. Although we don't really have a problem with carrot fly we usually protect our crops anyway by covering all the newly sown carrots with either fleece or enviromesh from the middle of May for about four weeks. The other defence we use against this pest is to grow resistant varieties such as carrot 'Maestro', which not only shows excellent resistance to carrot root fly but also to cavity spot and alternaria. Very often when varieties are bred to be resistant they lose some of their taste but not this variety and this makes it a must for any vegetable plot. My final choice is one of the new breed of coloured carrots. Apart from enhancing the look of any meal it also gives you the opportunity to surprise children and amaze your friends with purple carrots. The variety 'Purple Haze' keeps its colour even after cooking and to my great amazement, also has an excellent carrot flavour. As it is an F1 hybrid we get excellent vigour from the crop and against all odds, straight roots!

Carrot 'Purple Haze'

Endive 'Moss Curled'

A lovely plant that can be used as a replacement for lettuce in autumn and winter salads. We usually start to sow the seeds outside from April in succession so that they don't mature all at the same time. Since the leaves can be slightly bitter we also blanch some by covering individual plants with a pot to exclude the light. The very frilly texture of the leaves adds to the look of salads as well.

Kale 'Redbor' and 'Dwarf Green Curled'

This is an absolute must for people who want fresh vegetables during late winter and early spring. Both these varieties withstand the harsh winter weather very well. We will always grow 'Redbor' in our vegetable plot because of its amazing red-green leaves, a colour which seems to become more intense the colder the weather gets. 'Dwarf Green Curled' is an excellent variety for those with limited space because it does stay small and compact whilst producing an excellent crop of curly leaves. When picking always remember to go for the young, tasty leaves which are packed with vitamin C.

Kohl Rabi 'Lanro'

A very versatile vegetable that can be eaten cooked or raw and has a flavour that can only be described as a cross between a cabbage and a turnip. That may not sound desperately appetising to some but take my word for it, once tasted you will be adding these to your seed list each year. Kohl Rabi 'Lanro' doesn't seem to be widely available in supermarkets. However, they are easy to grow outside and need to be harvested when they get to about the size of a tennis ball and when they are still young and tender. I have to confess to picking, peeling and then eating them rather like an apple.

Leek 'Atal', 'Carlton' and 'Musselburgh'

I'm sure that we don't all want to be eating just brassicas through winter, lovely as they are because, as I keep telling Sue, variety is the spice of life! I have therefore chosen varieties that will give a very long harvesting period. 'Atal' is another baby vegetable and it is very well suited to being grown in multi-sown modules as well as cropped in raised beds. However, its main asset is that it can be harvested from summer onwards. We also use the variety 'Carlton' as a multi-sown crop although that is a bonus rather than the main reason for growing it. The stems on this high yielding variety are long, straight and absolutely delicious and we start to harvest the main crop from autumn. The variety we grow specifically for winter harvest is 'Musselburgh' which also has good long stems that have an excellent flavour but above all, are exceptionally winter hardy. One thing that we always ensure is that we

Leek 'Musselburgh'

have a small amount of leeks heeled in a trench so that when the ground is frosty and solid and difficult to dig there are always some leeks that can be used.

Lettuce 'Lollo Rosso', 'Jefferson', 'Valdor', 'Fristina' and 'Little Gem'

What an impossible task! Having to keep the selection of lettuce down to only five when there are so many fantastic varieties to choose from. We sow at least two varieties of lettuce outside every two weeks from March so that we have a continual supply. As I have already indicated, I like the look and texture of frilly leaves so I guess it's no surprise that the variety 'Lollo Rosso' is in my selection. The colourful deep red-tinged leaves add to the beauty of the vegetable plot as well as the salad bowl which is why we have it growing in our Ornamental Kitchen Garden every year. We tend to start them early and plant the first crop outside under cloches. Over recent years the iceberg lettuces have become very popular and in my opinion the variety 'Jefferson' is one of the best. It has rich green leaves that form into a dense, crisp head and they can be harvested from May onwards provided you sow early. To complement our endive we also grow the varieties 'Fristina' and 'Valdor'. 'Fristina' is very well suited to growing under protection so we always have enough plants in pots in our greenhouse right through the winter. 'Valdor' however is autumn sown and produces large, tight hearts that sit well through the winter for harvesting in spring. The final variety I have chosen is a cos type that is so adaptable it can be grown in containers, under cloches, in rows or in raised beds. It is only small, but is definitely worthy of the saying 'small is beautiful'. It is quick to mature and so can be used as a catch crop as well as a main crop with an excellent flavour. We like to start this variety in modules

raised in the greenhouse from a February sowing to be planted out under cloches and then sown every two weeks. We have them right through until the autumn, fantastic!

Melon 'Sweetheart' and 'Early Sweet'

This is a crop that we only grow in the greenhouses that can be viewed but not entered into. In the gardens we suffer from the 'if we only take one then they won't miss it' syndrome on things like tomatoes, apples, pears, plums, cucumbers, etc., but when it comes to melons, like my father before me, I get very possessive. We have found that the variety 'Sweetheart' produces fruit at a lower temperature than many of the other varieties so it can be grown outside under cloches if you don't have a greenhouse. 'Early Sweet' requires the protection of a greenhouse or polythene tunnel where it will produce a hefty crop of rounded fruits that have a very tasty salmon-pink flesh.

Melon 'Sweetheart'

Melon 'Early Sweet'

Pea 'Fortune' and 'Sugarbon'

There seem to be very few people these days who have the time or the inclination to sit and pod fresh peas, especially when they taste so good from a frozen packet. It is something I must confess that we do not do either. It's not that we don't want to or cannot be bothered with but simply because there are never any left to harvest! Not only do we pick a pod or two (just like the Artful Dodger) as we pass, but so do the rest of the staff. The taste is just out of this world and neither myself or Sue can stop ourselves from doing it – I wonder if there is counselling offered for this sort of addiction? We like to push the boundaries with our peas to get as early a crop as possible so we start the variety 'Fortune' in guttering in the greenhouse during December. Once hardened off they will be slid out of the guttering into a drill and covered with a cloche, guaranteeing a very early crop. The other variety that we grow is 'Sugarbon' because we like mange tout peas and they are always so expensive to buy. It is a dwarf plant and easy to grow and it produces a really heavy crop of sweet pods that are ideal for steaming, stir frying or raw in salads.

Pea 'Fortune'

Potato 'Swift', 'Cara', 'Maris Piper' and 'Salad Blue'

In the UK potato planting is traditionally carried out over the Easter Bank Holiday weekend, but at Barnsdale this is when we are lifting our first crop of new potatoes. We have a definite way with potatoes that gives us a crop that can be harvested continually from Easter right through the year, blight willing. Our first crop is produced in a hot box using the variety 'Swift', which we find produces the earliest crop of all the varieties we have tried. This is followed by another planting which is grown in large containers in the greenhouse. Our first three rows of 'earlies' are planted in the ground under clear polythene which gives us our next crop, followed by the first 'earlies' grown normally with no polythene cover. They are then naturally followed by the second 'earlies' and main crop varieties. Once lifted the main crop varieties are stored in a frost free, cool, dark place in paper sacks and used when required. Storing in this way usually means that we have potatoes available right up until we start cropping the hot box again. The two main crop varieties that we grow are 'Cara' and 'Maris Piper', mainly because they both have a wide range of uses in the kitchen and store very well.

Potato 'Swift'

Potato 'Salad Blue'

The other variety I have chosen is definitely my favourite but not because it has the best flavour or because it produces an excellent crop, as it doesn't really fulfil either of these categories. No, I like to grow this potato because it is blue! It has a blue skin just like other more well-known blue varieties, but unlike the others it has a blue flesh which remarkably stays blue even after cooking. Now if this variety of potato doesn't get children eating vegetables then I don't know what will. Can you imagine their faces when you appear at the table holding their plate consisting of bangers, peas, gravy and a pile of blue mash? All the other potatoes that we grow are obtained from our seed supplier as seed potato but the 'Salad Blue' had to be ordered from a specialist potato supplier as micro-propagated slips (young plants) that were grown on to produce a crop that year. We have also found that our slugs rather like the taste of this variety so we now grow them in large containers, in a slug-free zone.

Scorzonera 'Russian Giant'

An odd vegetable really that not many gardeners have heard of but one that we have been growing for about twenty years. You might think that it is relatively unknown because it is hard to grow but nothing could be further from the truth. Sow the seed thinly into drills outside during April and May and that is about as complicated as it gets. I find that the only problem I have with this crop is getting the long thin roots out of the ground. The black outer skin belies the white, delicately flavoured flesh beneath.

Sweet Corn 'Indian Summer', 'Sundance' and 'Minipop'

Probably the one thing that puts most gardeners off growing a crop of sweet corn is having harvested cobs that are only half full of kernels. This is due to lack of pollination and if it has happened to you then the answer is to grow your sweet corn in a block. Because these plants are wind pollinated, the wind will only pollinate them all if it blows directly down the row, whereas block planting gives you a better overall pollination irrespective of wind direction. 'Indian Summer' is listed as being a novelty variety because of its multi-coloured kernels and it's also a sweet, tender and high yielding variety. 'Sundance' is one of those varieties that will produce an excellent crop in our very variable climate, even doing well in the north of England. The difference between growing sweet corn yourself and buying it is in the freshness. The minute a cob has been removed from its stem the sugar in the kernels begins to turn to starch, so the greater the time between

Sweet Corn 'Indian Summer'

picking and eating the less sweet your cob will be. When Sue leaves work the first thing she does when she gets home is to put on a pan of boiling water and the last thing I do when I leave work is to go and pick the cobs so that there is only a matter of minutes between picking and cooking. In all honesty I have never tasted better sweet corn than the ones we grow ourselves. Being a lover of Chinese food and in particular stir fries, I could not be without the variety 'Minipop' which produces 7-10cm (3"-4") long cobs but unlike the other varieties which are harvested when the tassels turn brown, these are picked when the tassels begin to show so that all parts of the cob can be eaten.

Herbs

Basil 'Neapolitan'

This annual is a must in the kitchen and therefore a must in the garden. Sown in a greenhouse from February, it produces large, slightly puckered leaves that have an excellent flavour.

Chives 'Garlic'

We tend to grow this plant in the border as well as the herb garden because of its lovely white, rounded flower heads. The leaves are slightly wider than those of the common chives and they have a mild garlic flavour, which makes them ideal for cooked dishes or raw in salads. It's very easy to grow and as it is perennial it will keep growing year after year, only having to be divided from time to time when the clump gets too big for its spot. Although they can be sown directly outside from March, we sow ours into modules in the greenhouse, pot them into 7cm (3") pots and then plant them out once they have

rooted into the pot. We are then able to start harvesting the leaves from June.

Cliantro

Another annual, that is also known as Leaf Coriander or Chinese Parsley and is not as widely grown as it should be. Picked fresh the leaves can be used on poultry, fish and in Chinese or Latin American dishes. We grow ours in the greenhouse in pots so that the plants never really reach maturity but if they do ultimately flower and therefore set seed, the resulting seeds can be used to give a spicy flavour to various dishes including soups, stews and curries.

Garlic 'Solent Wight'

Although technically a herb, you will usually find this listed under the vegetable section of most seed catalogues. 'Solent White' is an excellent variety that will produce lovely large bulbs with an exquisite flavour. If you are worried about the after effects on your breath then chewing some fresh parley leaves will counter the garlic odour, leaving you able to enjoy the benefits of this beautiful herb. Plant out individual cloves any time from February to April for harvesting from July onwards. Always remember to grow enough so that you have plenty to dry and store for use over winter. Not only does this herb have a fantastic flavour, essential to any modern day kitchen, but it's also reputed to lower blood pressure and cholesterol levels as well as combating bacterial, fungal and viral infections.

Mint 'Spearmint', 'Variegated Applemint' and 'Ginger Mint'

These have so many culinary uses that no cook should be without them in their garden. The one big drawback with most mints is that they can take over the area where they are planted and so we plant our more vigorous varieties into several different containers around the gardens and only put the more easily controlled directly into the borders. 'Spearmint', as you would expect, has a clear spearmint flavour and can be used for mint sauce with new potatoes and peas, in drinks and salads. It is a vigorous variety so always grow it in a container and pick it on a regular basis to encourage the production of plenty of new, young, tasty shoots. Although it does not have a strongly flavoured leaf, we grow 'Variegated Applemint' because it also has excellent decorative values. The light green leaves have a distinctive creamy-white edge as well as a mild apple mint flavour. This variety is not as vigorous as some, although the leaves tend to last longer into winter than most, so we make the most of it and plant it in the borders. My final choice is 'Ginger Mint', which has a hint of spice in the leaf and also has excellent decorative uses in the garden with its fresh green leaves erratically splashed golden-yellow. It is one that needs to be picked or cut back regularly to encourage the younger growth that carries the brighter markings. It is moderately vigorous but still worth putting in the border. If you are still not convinced about the need for mints in the garden then bear in mind that they have cosmetic, household, aromatic, decorative and medicinal uses as well as their vast range of culinary uses, so surely all that now remains is to decide which of the hundred or so varieties to grow!

Mint 'Spearmint'

Mint 'Ginger Mint'

Parsley 'Plain Leaved' and 'Moss Curled'

A very versatile herb that is packed full of vitamins and nutrients. The germination of parsley is generally quite slow but we have found that this is greatly improved if the seeds are sprinkled with boiling water after sowing, because the high temperature helps to break the seed's dormancy. Both the varieties chosen have a good parsley taste although the variety 'Plain Leaved' has the stronger flavour, but 'Moss Curled' has a better decorative value. We grow both so that we have a choice depending on whether it is taste or the look we are after. At the end of October we lift some clumps of our 'Moss Curled' parsley and pot them into two litre pots which we then place in a cold greenhouse, enabling us to continue picking the parsley throughout the winter, irrespective of the weather.

Parsley 'Plain Leaved'   *Parsley 'Moss Curled'*

Rocket 'Wild'

A very easily grown annual herb that we start off in a greenhouse, sown in a length of guttering, just so that we can get a really early crop. The peppery taste and deeply cut leaves really give salads a lift. It's a crop that will re-grow once cut so there is no real need for successive sowings. As with other herbs, we sow some late, into pots, so we can be cutting and enjoying the leaves well into the winter.

Fruit

```
31-08-2009

3......17·99
3.......5·00
3.......3·99
*.....26·98ST
*.....26·98TL
*.....26·98CA
     143668
14·08      00
```

Apple 'Egremont Russet', 'Queen Cox' and 'Bramley'

Depending on the training methods you use, fruit trees do not have to take up much space in the garden and there surely cannot be anything better than picking fresh fruit straight from the garden. The apple 'Egremont Russet' is my personal favourite but it's not to everyone's taste. It has a thickish skin with distinctive russet-bronze and crisp flesh that has a rich, nutty taste all its own. It's also an excellent cropper that is self-fertile, so there's no need for a pollinator, and fruits picked in October will last until January in store. If that was my personal favourite then 'Cox's Orange Pippin' has to be the nation's favourite, but the problem is that it does not grow well in most areas of the UK. However, all is not lost because those clever breeders have come up with a variety called 'Queen Cox', which not only grows well all over the place, but is self-fertile to boot. It still has that typical 'Cox' flavour, is sweet and juicy and the way to tell the two types apart is that it has a deeper red flush on the skin. As with 'Egremont Russet' this is a good variety for a smaller garden as you don't need a pollinator. We now move from the nation's favourite eater to the nation's favourite cooker, the 'Bramley'. At Barnsdale we have now started planting the fantastically named and greatly improved form called 'Clone 20'. The reason it's so greatly improved is that, historically, the main problem with this apple variety was the vigour, which was too much for the increasing amount of smaller gardens to cope with. This new form has reduced the vigour, which means that it's able to put more effort into producing a bigger crop of enormous apples. Unlike the other varieties in this section, it is not self-fertile and needs at least two pollinators but is definitely worth it as they can be picked from October and will store really well through the winter.

Blueberry

I am a fairly recent convert to blueberries, not because I didn't like them, just that I hadn't got round to trying them until my father had a blueberry producer on 'Gardeners' World'. The chap arrived clutching a blueberry cheesecake and needless to say my lunchtime was not only an education but heavenly. This variety is compact and therefore very suited to growing in a pot, which is an important feature for this soft fruit. They like to be grown in an acid soil so for those of us who cannot supply this in the garden, a container is the only answer. Potted into an ericaceous mix it will produce lovely white flowers in the spring followed by large clusters of juicy blueberries during July and August. If this isn't enough, they then produce a spectacular autumn colour before the leaves fall in the autumn. Definitely a plant that satisfies both the ornamental gardener as well as the productive gardener.

Fig 'Brown Turkey'

My mother had a thing for dried figs and I just couldn't bring myself to try them so I avoided eating the fruit my father offered me from his 'Brown Turkey'. Then one day when nobody was looking I pinched one and took the smallest bite just to see if his description of the difference between fresh and dried figs was true. As much as I hate to admit it, he had hit the nail right on the head. There is definitely no comparison between the juicy, sweet red flesh of a freshly picked fig and those dried up lumps you buy from the shops. The variety 'Brown Turkey' is probably the most reliable for our climate and does exceptionally well on a south or west facing wall and in the poorest soil you can give it. If you plant your fig in good soil it will grow magnificently but produce very little fruit, which is why they grow so well against walls because they are generally planted in poor soil directly over the wall foundations. If you are planting against a fence and you think your soil may be too good then put a paving slab at the bottom of the hole and place the plant directly on top of it. With our shorter summers it will produce small figs one year that will ripen the following summer so in the winter it's worth giving the bush some sort of protection. We cover ours with fleece once the weather starts to turn frosty and leave it on all winter.

Kiwi Fruit 'Jenny'

This is not the juiciest or the largest of the kiwi fruit varieties but it is self-fertile so there is no need for a pollinator, which makes it ideally suited to smaller gardens. We have a male form growing as an ornamental climber on one of our pergolas and it's so vigorous that it completely takes it over each summer. The variety 'Jenny' is nowhere near as vigorous and produces an excellent crop of smallish fruits in late summer. An added bonus is the red-tipped growth produced as the leaves emerge in the spring. To get the best out of this variety it is advisable to grow it on a south-facing, sheltered wall.

Plum 'Victoria'

Without doubt the most well known and best loved of all the plums and gages. It produces staggering crops of sweet, juicy, green-purple plums during August that are best when eaten whilst standing right next to the tree! If you can control yourself and manage to take some fruit to the kitchen it's great for making jam and in pies. 'Victoria' can be quite vigorous so it's best to get them on a 'Victoria' semi-dwarfing rootstock such as St. Julian 'A' which will give a very manageable tree of about 2-2.5m (6'-8') high. It is important to stop the branches of the tree becoming overly congested. Once the tree is established, annual pruning is recommended but only when the tree starts to burst into growth in the spring as this minimises the risk of silver leaf. This disease is becoming more prevalent and infects the tree through open wounds, which is why pruning should be carried out when the tree has the ability to heal any cuts very quickly. The one drawback of this variety is that it can behave in a biennial manner sometimes. If you have an outrageously good crop one year the tree will very often take a breather in the following year, producing only a handful of fruit before coming back with a vengeance the year after.

Raspberry 'Autumn Bliss'

Without doubt the best tasting of all raspberries. It's always listed as an autumn fruiting variety because you will be picking the fruit right up until the first frosts but it starts producing fruit for harvest from late July! With all autumn fruiting varieties the fruit is produced on the current year's canes so at the end of the year all the canes are cut down to the ground. This spineless variety produces an excellent crop of fruit that freezes really well if you can't get through them all at the first attempt. As we grow ours in a 120cm (4') wide bed we find it pays to support the outside canes with wire or string to prevent them flopping over under the weight of the crop and ruining the fruit.

Strawberry 'Flamenco' and 'Mae'

If you are after strawberry plants that will fruit all summer then look no further than the variety 'Flamenco'. This British bred variety produces large, bright red fruit that not only have a delicious flavour but are also produced in abundance. We like to grow this variety in conjunction with 'Mae', which gives us a very early crop and extends the season. 'Mae' is another British bred variety that will start to produce ripe, large, juicy fruit from the beginning of June. With these two varieties combined we can start the run up to Wimbledon early and continue celebrating a British win with strawberries and cream until the end of August! (Or drown our sorrows with champagne and strawberries.)

Strawberry 'Mae'

Barnsdale's Own Gardeners'
Question Time - Part 3

Gardeners' Questions answered by Nick and Sue.

Adrian Lisecki lives in Bedford. He would like to know how do you define Soil Sickness and what is it? How can it be noticed? Is there any way to prevent it? And is there a long time solution to this problem if it exists?

I have spoken to many old timers who say that they have never heard of it, yet swear by the frequent feeding of Tonks Formula / Mixture! However many Garden Centres are completely lost when you mention this feed! Rose replant disease, as it is known, is a problem that affects the roots of roses. The most common and noticeable symptoms are poor shoot growth and stunting. It occurs in soil where roses have already been grown. If you have an old bush that has seen better days and you wish to replace it with another rose there is a good chance that the new plant will succumb to the disease. The general consensus of opinion is that harmful pathogens build up around the roots of roses as they establish and, as the plant gets older, the pathogens increase. When you plant a rose with only a minimal root system into a soil full of pathogens it does not stand much of a chance. Although the disease happens in most cases where one rose replaces another it doesn't always occur but the risk is so great that prevention is better than cure. The pathogens can be eradicated by treating the soil where the rose has been with a proprietary soil steriliser or, as we do, by digging out the soil around where our rose was and swapping it with soil from another part of the garden where roses have not been growing. These pathogens only affect plants in the Rosaceae family which includes roses, apples and plums. As far as we are aware Tonks Formula is a general term for rose fertilizer which will obviously boost rose growth.

Noreen Dyer from Croughton. Asks what depth should Eremurus be planted?

At Barnsdale we plant ours around 15cm (6") deep. They like a well drained position so if you garden on heavy clay soil it is a good idea to improve it with garden compost and coarse grit.

Alison Burch from Lincoln. Wants to know how she can get Asparagus to grow in heavy clay soil.

Asparagus likes a free draining soil so you will need to grow it in a raised bed where the soil has been enhanced with compost and coarse grit. The combination of these two elements will give the asparagus the drainage it requires to grow and crop well.

Noel Oakwell from Leicester. Says that she has a Blackcurrant bush that is looking tired and past its best, can she propagate from it or should she buy a new plant?

There is no need to splash out on a new plant because Blackcurrants are easy to propagate from hardwood cuttings. Once the bush has lost its leaves find a strong and healthy stem, about the thickness of a pencil and cut it to about 20cm (8") in length. This can then be inserted into prepared soil and will root by the following autumn.

Mark Wood in Manchester. Wants to know why the tender perennials in his garden always rot off in the winter, he says that he feeds and waters them well.

It sounds as if you may be giving them too much water, Mark. These plants like to be kept just above the point of wilting during winter and early spring as they will rot off very quickly if too much water is applied.

Johanna Newman from Luton. Says that she is in the process of building a wormery and that her friend has advised her not to buy expensive worms for it but to dig them out of the garden, is this good advice?

Unfortunately garden worms will not do as good a job on your waste material as brandling worms will. These are the variety of worms you should use in a wormery. Don't buy them from specialists as they can be obtained much cheaper from your local fishing tackle shop.

Ted Williams in North Norfolk. Says that he is a keen organic gardener and wants to know how to combat cabbage root fly.

If you are not already great friends with the man in your local carpet shop then you should be, because the remedy is simple and involves a freebie from the carpet shop man. Ask for any off-cuts of carpet underlay he has lying around in the back of the shop, take it home and cut it into 10cm (4") squares. And cut a slit from one side into the centre. When you plant your brassicas slot this mat snugly around your plants so that the adult cabbage root fly cannot lay her eggs next to the brassica stem. These mats can be reused for several years.

Sue Harwell in Tewkesbury. Wants to know the best way to keep houseplants watered whilst she is away on holiday.

We have found that bribing a neighbour with the promise of a lovely gift on our return usually works! Failing that, place your plants on a piece of capillary matting situated on the draining board and immerse the end into a sink full of water. The plants draw the water they require out of the matting and the matting tops itself up by drawing water from the sink. This method prevents the plants from becoming overly wet.

May Eastwell who lives in Kent. Has a Rochester fan trained peach tree, on a west facing wall, it flowers but never sets any fruit, why is this?

Peaches are self fertile, so it will not be a fertility problem. It sounds very much like the flowers are being frosted. It is important to protect the flowers or young fruit if there is a frost forecast. We use horticultural fleece which is light and easy to attach and will keep out about two degrees of frost.

Fred Winter from Didsbury. Says that he visited Barnsdale and saw home grown, new potatoes in October! He wants to know how to achieve this in his garden.

Once our first early potatoes have been lifted we pick out some unblemished tubers and replant them outside. Covered in straw from the first frost these will be ready and can be lifted for serving with the Christmas turkey.

Margaret Thompson in Bedford. Likes to use coloured wood chip in her garden but finds that it fades very quickly. Do you have any tips?

There are two basic tips. The first is to buy blue coloured recycled glass that will not fade or, if you wish to stick to wood, we have found a beech chip that is impregnated with a coloured dye and then kiln dried. In our Mediterranean Garden it has been on a pathway for 18 months and shows no signs of fading. The company that we acquired it from is called 'Chipwright' and they are based near York, although it should be available through good garden centres.

Nell from West Norwood. Wants to know when would be the best time to divide Asters.

With all herbaceous perennials the time to divide is anytime from the autumn, once the plant has begun to die back, right through until the spring, when it just starts to shoot. We will usually divide at either end so that we have a guide as to what we are doing by using the old stems to guide us or, indeed, the new shoots.

June Stanton who lives in Northchurch, Hertfordshire. Asks is there an easy way to propagate my monster spider plant?

Yes, just pin one of the small plantlets, which are to be found at the end of the plant's long, leg-like stems, into a pot of propagation compost and it will root in 2-4 weeks.

George Arthur from Hertfordshire. Has been told that damping down the floor in his greenhouse during the summer is important and he wants to know why he has been advised to do this.

During summer a greenhouse can get very hot and damping down the floor helps to cool it down. When the water evaporates it also adds moisture to the air. This prevents the plants from losing too much water and saves you the trouble of watering more often.

Phyllis in Bedfordshire. Says that she knows Leylandii are not everybody's favourite but, in order to keep hers under control, when is the best time to trim them?

At Barnsdale we have a short Leylandii hedge, half in green and half in gold and we trim it twice a year with mechanical hedge cutters. The first cut is in June to tidy the first flush of growth, with the second being in September when we give it a last tidy up to see it through the winter.

Sylvia Smith in Baldock. I keep hearing about buying Snowdrops 'in the green', why?

Snowdrops dry out very quickly when they are out of the ground so the success rate from bought, dried bulbs can be erratic. However, buying them in leaf, or 'in the green', ensures that the bulbs you are planting are definitely alive.

Ray in Letchworth. Loves Jerusalem artichokes and would like to grow them but the last time he tried they did their best to take over his vegetable plot! What could he do to prevent this happening?

They are a much underused vegetable in my opinion Ray, but you are right they can be a bit of a beast. If given the space, in a windy garden, they make an excellent hedge but need to be controlled every year with a spade along the edge. We grow ours in large containers that, if necessary, can be sunk into the ground and pulled up when we need to harvest the tubers.

Mrs. A. Clark lives in the East Midlands. She has inherited three, very tall and somewhat overgrown Lilac trees. Can they be cut down to a reasonable size and will they flower again.

It is possible to rejuvenate an overgrown lilac by cutting it back hard to within 45cm (18") of the ground. This is a drastic measure and should be spread over 2-3 years. Take out one half or a third each year. The pruning needs to be carried out after flowering. Your lilac will flower again, although it may take the hump and miss a couple of years before it starts again.

Pauline Alstead from Kettering. Wants to know how many different colours and varieties of dogwood are available.

There are over 30 different varieties of Cornus alba, sanguinea and sericea (stolonifera) that are commonly known as dogwoods. These come in a range of colours and shades of yellow, green, orange, red and purple, the leaves are sometimes variegated and also come in many different shades of green.

Mrs. Beverley Cross lives near Saffron Walden in Essex. And asks is it a good idea to replace a Laurel bush which has been in our front drive for some years, with Yew trees. Will they grow under the same conditions?

Yes, is the simple answer, but when removing a large plant and replacing it with something else remember to improve the soil with organic matter and some fertiliser before planting.

J. Taylor from Taunton. Would like you to recommend some drought happy plants.

An excellent rule of thumb is to look for succulent leaf plants as these have the capabilities of resisting drought conditions, one of the more well known ones being Sedum. These come in a range of types from perennial border plants right through to delicate alpine plants. Aucuba, Berberis, Elaeagnus, Ajuga and Ilex will also do well. Sempervivums and Euphorbia characias are also very good, as are grey leaved plants such as Cistus, Oleander, Lavender and Hebe.

Anne Stevman from Kent. Is concerned about global warming and wants to know if she should make any adjustments to the way she gardens.

Gardeners, traditionally, are very adaptable people and we will adapt with our planting as the weather dictates. We are already finding that certain tender plants are regularly surviving British winters without any protection. This trend seems set to continue and we will adjust with it. Of greater concern is the likelihood of less water becoming available. Make sure that you attach water butts to every available down pipe, shed and greenhouse.

Howard Cross is from Tiptree. He would like some tips on growing vegetables in clay soil.

We have been doing this for the last 23 years at Barnsdale. Each year we add well rotted organic matter such as farm yard manure or garden compost to our vegetable plot. We struggle sometimes with root crops but even these now grow well. So the long and short of it is that if you keep adding organic matter you will improve the structure and drainage of your soil.

Emma Rothery in Buckinghamshire. Asks how do I get rid of black spots on Hellebore leaves?

It sounds like you, or more precisely your hellebores, are suffering from leaf spot. These appear as dark brown or black spots, mainly on the younger foliage. It can be controlled by initially removing the infected leaves and burning them, this will prevent its spread to healthy leaves. You could try spraying with Bordeaux mixture at the given rate throughout the winter/early spring, but not during the period when the plant begins to send up flower buds.

Mrs. C. Clements gardens near Sevenoaks. And she has a small garden which means that she has to keep her firethorn under control, she cuts it back more than once a year. Can you recommend the best times, so that it still produces berries for the birds?

Pyracantha or firethorn as it is commonly known, flowers quite early so it can be cut back to within 2-3 leaves from the previous year's growth. This will not affect the berries as they are forming on the growth produced the previous year. It is then possible to lightly trim to keep it under control bearing in mind that you will need to allow some growth each year for berries the following year. To help keep your plant under control you can also remove some shoots in late winter or early spring to allow space for younger shoots to grow in.

Part Four - Containers and Patios

If Nick is good at hitting his thumb with a hammer then Sue is simply great at planting containers. I had a really conservative approach towards containers in the garden before I met Sue. You know the sort of thing, in the summer the odd geranium surrounded by some lobelia and maybe a bit of alyssum, very artistic, I don't think! In this section Sue will explain how to use all kinds of plants to create a horticultural work of art. You will find out how to get the best out of your plants both in the garden and in containers because you can utilise them in both.

I love containers because it is possible not only to change the mood but also the feeling of a garden with the introduction of a few strategically placed pots, whatever the time of year. Unlike the permanent planting in a garden that may be moved once in its life, containers can be not only replanted to give a different effect for summer, winter and spring, but also the sheer act of moving pots around will give a completely different look. I never take my planting too seriously, as I like to experiment and play on the basis that there are no real do's and don'ts when it comes to containers.

Mind you, saying that, there are two or three essentials to bear in mind. Firstly, any container you have planted is totally dependent on your care and attention for its survival. Given the right watering and feeding, the pots, troughs and baskets that you have laboured over will reward you with a wonderful display. Secondly, the interest period you are planting for is very important as this will dictate the type of container you must use. If your container is made from clay and will be outside during very cold weather then it must be marked as 'frost proof', as 'frost resistant' pots, though fine for summer planting, will only last a couple of years if subjected to harsh weather.

The next point to bear in mind is what you want to plant. Is it an acid lover such as a Rhododendron, Acer, Erica, etc? Does it prefer a free draining compost? Or has it another particular requirement of the growing medium? The type of compost used is a really important factor to be considered before planting up any container. One thing that many gardeners forget to take into account is that the taller the plant or plants, the heavier the compost will need to be otherwise the planted container may be blown over and damaged. I like to use a variety of different sizes of container, to add interest, and sometimes I add ballast to the bottom of pots to make them more stable, such as bricks, stones or gravel. However, if your pocket will stretch that far, pots and troughs made from lead will need no ballast as they will inevitably be heavy enough. Just try lifting one and you will see what I mean. Fibreglass or plastic imitations, although usually very realistic, lack the all important weight factor, as do terracotta and stone reproductions. I have found that visiting reclamation yards is usually a good source of stone and lead troughs and sometimes more elaborate pots that come already weatherbeaten and antique-looking so that when placed in the garden they look as if they have always been there.

One of the great benefits of container gardening is that pots and hanging baskets can be hung on walls and fences, giving a great opportunity, when a lot of the herbaceous plants have died down in the garden, to get interest back at eye level. If necessary I use not only bedding but also herbaceous plants and shrubs. These may only have a two year life in my containers but once their usefulness has been exhausted I can then plant them in the gardens and enjoy them for years to come, or give them away to friends or family without much pain to the pocket!

I like my pots to stand out because of what is in them and not because they look too shiny and new, so when I repot the container it is only cleaned if it is too dirty. A bit of algae looks good as it makes the container fade into the background, therefore promoting the plants to the fore. Trailing plants are also useful to achieve this effect.

I propose to look at containers for two seasons – summer/autumn and winter/spring to cover a full year.

Choosing your containers

For the containers to be used on the patio I have made use of pots constructed from a lightweight man-made material, as well as terracotta. The man-made pots come in a good range of colours as well as being completely frost proof so I can use them for summer or winter colour and they are so light that moving the pots around from time to time is made very easy.

It is sometimes more difficult to move wall pots around as they will inevitably come with a slightly different fixing for each pot. This means that once planted and positioned on the wall they will stay in that place for the whole season.

There is no need to stick to traditional containers when looking to add spice, quirkiness or just something different to your garden. As with the plants, I like to experiment with less traditional types of container as well as using materials that relate to the area they are going in to. A couple of years ago I caught our head gardener Jon attempting to throw away his old work boots that had acquired at least one hole in each sole. All I could see were two perfect containers for seasonal plants and the holes meant that I didn't even have to ask Nick to drill me a drainage outlet. For the winter I like to use a Hellebore x ericsmithii, with its large pink-flushed white flowers, in one and Erica x darleyensis 'Spring Surprise' in the other as its mass of dark pink

flowers picks out the pink in the hellebore. These boots were then positioned at the end of the pathway in the allotment, just outside the shed as if they had been taken off after a long hard day, and have raised several eyebrows and generated plenty of comments since.

Another home for plants I like to utilise is naturally occurring and perfect for Sempervivums. I am sure that most of us can get hold of a branch or log, and either will make the perfect home for this very easy plant. A short, fat log stood on end with its top scooped out very roughly, so that it looks natural, can be filled with a small amount of gritty compost before squeezing in the Sempervivums. If you already have some of these plants in your garden, they are easy to propagate so take some rosettes as cuttings, root them and use these in your log or branch as they will be much easier to insert. I have used several different varieties and have dug out holes for the plants at different levels to give more interest. Once they form offsets and these begin to hang, the effect will become even more dramatic. A single branch can be just as effective, but look for one with plenty of gnarls and knobbles on it as it is these areas scooped out that will give the most natural effect. As these plants will grow in sun or semi-shade we have used our log and branch on the edge of woodland where they both look as if they have fallen and the Sempervivums have grown onto them. These evergreen rosettes look fantastic all year round, so once in place they do not need to be changed each season. Another excellent range of plants that will suit this style of growing are the heathers, but remember, if you are using summer flowering varieties they need an ericaceous compost to grow in. If you grow summer flowering and winter flowering heathers in two different logs or branches they can be interchanged to suit their flowering times.

This next container, I have to admit, was not my idea. Nick sprinted over to me with what he thought was an inspirational brainwave for a demonstration we had been asked to perform, on growing vegetables in containers. He wanted to grow leeks in a bed pan so that he could finish our demonstration by producing this bed pan whilst saying, "Have you ever woken up in the night in desperate need of a leek?" I know it is sad, but I just humour him - well, you have to, don't you? Anyway, there is no reason why a drainage hole cannot be drilled into the bottom of it and used, but I would suggest very colourful summer bedding or something more subtle such as alpines, instead of Nick's idea! However, it is possible to grow a wide range of vegetables in containers if you do not have space in the

garden, live in a flat or just want to force crops, such as early new potatoes, carrots, lettuce, rocket, etc.

You could, of course, make your own containers using hypertufa. This is a coir, sand and cement mix that we have used extensively to make rocks for our alpine features as well as sink-like containers for alpines, bedding plants and vegetables. Before giving our most recently made trough over to alpines we have positioned it in the Ornamental Kitchen Garden and sown a quick crop of leaf salad. The great advantages of these types of container are that they are frost proof, easy to make, fairly light to lift and look fantastic when planted up. What more could you want? And just think of the satisfaction when people admire it, having to admit not only that you made it yourself but also grew all the plants yourself, how home-made is that?

Preparing your containers

The first thing to ensure when buying a container is that it has ample drainage holes. With smaller wall pots you can get away with one, whilst the larger standing pots require more drainage, therefore more holes at the bottom. I must admit to having being tempted, more than once, with a lovely looking container with only one drainage hole, when it required at least three, and then having to secretly get the drill out when I got home. If careful, it is possible with a good drill and a masonry bit to make as many drainage holes in the bottom of terracotta pots as is required. But, be warned, things do not always proceed as planned! Wooden containers and ones made from man-made materials are obviously much easier to drill without fear of breakage.

When you are satisfied with the amount of drainage holes in your pot, the next stage is to ensure they do not become blocked. This is achieved by the use of crocks. A crock is usually a broken piece of terracotta pot that is placed over the hole, allowing excess water to drain away. If you are better with a drill than I am and therefore do not have any broken pots, large stones are a good substitute. It is also possible to buy products from the garden centre to do the same job, but this can get quite expensive. The added bonus of a crock is that it will prevent the compost in the pot from falling out.

For winter containers I like to use a gritty compost for good drainage and so that the pot will not get waterlogged, even during wetter spells. The opposite is the case for summer containers as water is at a premium and watering may have to be done at least twice a day, so it pays to keep as much in the pot as possible. I have found that water-holding gel added to the compost at the filling stage works very well as it swells and stores water when the compost is wetted for the plants to draw on later. It does give a bit of a safety net if I get carried away enjoying a sunny day in the garden and miss one watering! When planting a permanent container I prefer to use a combination of winter and summer compost, something that has some drainage for the winter, but not so much that it dries out too quickly in the summer, although I find shrubs require slightly less water than summer bedding, which tends to gulp up as much water as you can fit into the pot. Because the container will be standing all year round, the compost needs to be a bit meatier than just a proprietary make and equal parts of garden soil, a proprietary compost and coarse grit give me everything that I need. If you are still worried about the possibility of poor drainage then it may help to lift pots off the ground with the use of pot feet.

The addition of soil to a hanging basket mix is not usually wise, unless you are in training for a weight lifting contest or have a bracket as substantial as the Eiffel Tower! For summer baskets, firstly I line my basket with wool that has been dyed green and works very well as a moss substitute. Then I place a square of polythene at the bottom of the basket to act as a well and, another moisture conservation essential, add the water-holding granules to the multipurpose compost, before half filling the basket with this mix. To make life easier and prevent damage to my beautifully grown plants I sit the basket onto a pot, raising it from the work surface so that it is at a better height to work on and stop it rolling around. I can then insert trailing plants through the wool and onto the compost, adding more compost as I go, ensuring that it is well packed around the roots of my plants. From painful experience I would suggest that you check the fixings of your bracket and if they are not completely secure, remedy it now or you will wake up one summer's morning to find your basket on the ground, bedding plants scattered all over your patio and a gaping hole where there was once a beautiful display.

If you get the basics right, such as the type of container, the compost, etc and then play with all sorts of plants and combinations, you will be surprised what you can come up with.

Summer/Autumn

These are my favourite seasons of the year because there is so much plant and colour choice available and I can let my imagination run riot. When I can, I use plug plants, primarily because there is an extensive range available these days. It is also much cheaper than buying bedding plants in pots leaving me with more money for other projects or even more pots! Plugs can be bought small, early on in the season, potted up and grown on a window sill, in a frost free greenhouse or conservatory. I have found that planting up containers at the end of April or in early May will produce a fairly full pot or basket by the beginning of June, when I can put them out without much fear of frost. I tend not to stick to any real pattern because some containers will be fairly simple, with just a couple of types of plants, while others will be packed to bursting point with many different varieties and a wide range of colours.

I always make sure that I have colour from the base upwards so I have planted pots to stand on the ground, pots to hang from a wall or fence, baskets to hang higher than the wall pots and a pouch to hang where ever I can find a space.

It is important, in any container, to have various height levels so, in the large terracotta pot I have used three plants of Argyranthemum 'Jamaica Snowstorm', a tender perennial in the centre surrounded by a combination of Arctosis 'Hannah' and New Guinea Impatiens 'White'. The Arctosis and Impatiens will tumble over the edge of the pot and the Argyranthemum will provide a continual display of white, daisy-

like flowers. In the round homemade coir pot I have mixed permanent planting with bedding by using the evergreen perennial Heuchera 'Silver Scrolls' as the centrepiece and the New Guinea Impations 'Salmon' as the contrast around the edge of the container.

Be daring and try different types of pots, for example, an aluminium container can look stunning with the right planting. I have used a tall, shiny pot with a Cordyline for height surrounded by a dark red Sempervivum, making it very modern and sophisticated. There are no bright colours in this pot but the architectural value on its own or in a group with other, more colourful pots, is outstanding. In groups I also use different coloured pots to contrast with, or to complement the planting.

Whilst in the mode of looking for something a little bit different I have also used a pouch, which is basically a long bag with holes cut into the sides. It is for hanging on a fence, wall, to cover a pipe, washing line post, etc, to produce a vertical column of colour. It is simple and easy to use, just fill it with compost and pop the plants into the side pockets, water well and hang in position.

Don't just use plants that are purely good to look at, why not plant up containers that give interest throughout the summer and are useful as well? Herbs can be planted in a wide range of containers, but I have used a wall pot in this instance. In the top there is parsley, chives, Eau de Cologne mint and nasturtium seeds pushed in between and around the sides. I have

also used more decorative thymes that can be used in the kitchen, 'Hartington Silver', 'Doone Valley' and doerfleri 'Bressingham'.

In the small wall pot I have planted the top with a mixture of white geranium and Begonia 'Illumination Mix' whilst the side pockets have been filled with Polygonum 'Pink Bubbles' which will cascade to give a tremendous effect. I have taken a bit of a chance as I am not sure exactly what colours the Begonias will be! But I am pretty sure that they will complement the white geranium. In the other pot I have substituted the white geranium with a salmon-pink one and replaced the Begonia with New Guinea Impatiens 'White'.

A larger wall container such as a trough gives me scope to be slightly more adventurous. Here the main upright planting consists of Osteospermums, 'Whirlygig' in the centre flanked by 'Mary'. These are

then surrounded by Petunia Surfinia 'Sky Blue', with Petunia Surfinia 'Velvet' being pushed into the sides, through the fake moss lining. This is ideal for a hot area, with the colours making it feel cool. While this is a horizontal burst of colour for a fence or a wall we can also have columnar cascades of colour by using a pouch. The top of this cascade of colour begins with an upright zonal geranium salmon-pink which is surrounded by New Guinea Impatiens White. The slits down the pouch are planted with Polygonum 'Pink Bubbles', Helichrysum 'Silver' and the 'Gold' variety and Petunia Surfinia 'Sky Blue' and 'Velvet'.

When it comes to hanging baskets I like to cram as much in as I can for maximum effect. I have used a Fuchsia Turkish Delight as the main central plant, which will look fantastic with its gorgeous, large violet-blue flowers and pink sepals, surrounded by white Geranium,

mixed Begonia and white Petunia Surfinia, with 'Velvet' Petunia Surfinia pushed in around the sides which will complement the colour of the Fuchsia. In the other basket I have used just red Geraniums as the central feature with Begonia surrounding them and the gold Helichrysum on the edge to tumble down which will contrast spectacularly with the red Surfinia Petunia pushed into the sides of the basket.

Winter/Spring

When planting a wall pot the larger plug plants are ideal as they need to be crammed into fairly small openings in the sides of the container, and give the best of both worlds, being reasonably cheap, but big enough to give an instant impact to the container. The wall pot I am planting here for winter interest is hand-made and frost proof, with a large opening at the top and three small pockets on the side. These will give me the opportunity to enjoy a good burst of colour at a more difficult time of year whilst covering up most of the pot, so that the plants are the main focus and not the container.

To give winter and spring interest, an evergreen Gaultheria has been used as the main focal point. On either side of this I have used small-leaved, evergreen Euonymus japonicus 'Microphyllus' to give balanced height. The red Polyanthus gives a nice splash of colour whilst picking up the red tints in the Gaultheria leaves. Gaultheria procumbens gives an extended season as the plant is covered with shiny red berries in the late autumn/early winter, which the birds usually devour. However, if you are in a more bird-free area, the fruits can last on the plant until spring. I don't mind feeding the birds because the glossy green leaves take on reddish tinges in the cold, so adding extra interest to my pot, and if crushed these leaves give off a fragrance of wintergreen. In the late spring/early summer this plant will be covered with whitish, pendulous, urn-shaped flowers. The trailing Ivy breaks up some of the starkness of the pot as well as adding brightness with its cream variegation. Lastly, I have used winter flowering Pansies in the small pockets on the sides in colours that complement the terracotta of the pot. All of these plants can be used in other types of

containers to great effect.

To achieve a slightly different feel just substitute one or two plants. I have again used nice little evergreens, which will give interest throughout the winter and spring. At the back the Euonymus japonicus 'Microphyllus' has been replaced by the very bright yellow and green leaves of Euonymus fortunei radicans 'Emerald and Gold'. In between these I have used a dwarf Narcissus to give a boost in late winter/early spring. At the front there is a Pieris 'Little Heath Green', which has interesting small green leaves in winter that, if cold enough, take on reddish tints and are then topped by numerous bell-shaped white flowers in spring. The variegated Ivy is still in place to break up the potential view of too much pot. As I have used some acid-loving plants in these two containers the compost is an ericaceous one, which the other plants will also grow perfectly happily in.

These varieties are also just as much at home in a larger container, such as a half barrel. The Pieris, Ivy, Heather and Fern tie in well with the timber theme as they give the whole container a real woodland feel. To add to the colour I have used Primroses and winter flowering Pansies. A simple trough containing Euonymus fortunei radicans 'Emerald Gaiety' and Primroses, with dwarf Narcissus to follow, is very effective for a darker spot and continuing the simple theme, just Primroses and Ivy in a small pot makes an excellent table decoration for those sunnier spring days.

As these are mostly plants that can be used in the garden, once their time in my wall pots has come to an end, it means that there are many different varieties that can be tried. I often use dwarf conifers, such as Chamaecyparis lawsoniana 'Elwood's Gold' or, my special favourite, Juniperus communis 'Compressa', both of which can be bought small enough to be used in a pot. Evergreen shrubs are now sold by garden centres in variety packs, giving a good selection of seasonal plants in small pots.

For the north aspect of our building I have two containers that are filled with plants that not only cope with such a cold spot but also perform well in shade. The first container has two Euphorbia amygdaloides 'Purpurea' at the back, which will give excellent purple foliage colour, complemented in the spring by the yellow-green flower bracts. To break up this purple backdrop I have used a dwarf daffodil, Narcissus 'Tete a Tete', with the early spring burst of yellow flowers contrasting perfectly with the leaves of the Euphorbia. In the front of the pot I have planted a winter flowering heather, Erica carnea 'Springwood Pink', surrounded on each side by the large lavender and yellow flowers of winter Pansies. This wall pot will give interest to a dull wall for the whole winter, right through until late spring.

The second north-facing, smaller wall pot has an Uncinia rubra at the back with Primula lilacena 'Flore Pleno' and Primula 'Sunshine Susie' filling the space in front. These double, winter/spring flowering primulas are old varieties and very much underused in the garden both in the border and in containers. 'Sunshine Susie' with its lovely bright yellow flowers always makes me smile, irrespective of how cold it is. Finally, I have used a trailing ivy, Hedera helix 'Glacier', to take the eye downwards and therefore expand the area of interest.

Barnsdale's Own Gardeners' Question Time - Part 4

Alison Blickerton from Northamptonshire. Has a Camellia in a pot on a patio which faces southwest. It is planted in ericaceous compost, has healthy leaves and has had lots of buds in autumn. In May some buds open but a great deal simply turn brown and fall off, any explanation?

The symptoms you have described make your problem sound like one of two things. It could be frost damage or the plant is suffering from lack of water. If it is possibly frost then you might try covering with horticultural fleece during cold nights or, if you think it might be lack of water, then the remedy is obvious. Many gardeners do not realize how quickly pots dry out, even when the sun does not shine!

Margaret Darlington from Leesthorpe, Leicestershire. Wants to know if she can plant potatoes that you buy from the supermarket and then begin shooting in her vegetable basket at home.

Buying your seed potatoes from a reputable supplier will minimize the risk of disease and you really cannot guarantee this if the source of supply is unknown. Also there are varieties available in supermarkets that do not grow well in our climate so it is best to buy the real thing and stop being so mean Margaret!

Ian McKay, Matlock, Derbyshire. Wants some suggestions for the care of a newly planted peach tree being trained along a south facing wall.

The first thing to do is to feed your tree in its early years until it is old enough to start bearing fruit (at about four years old). In spring protect the blossoms when frost is forecast, woven horticultural fleece is ideal for this. Remember that, as they flower early, they may need to be hand pollinated; this is because it could be too early for flying insects to do the job for you. Once trained and beginning to fruit the peach is pruned twice a year. In summer allow the side-shoots to grow up to 4-6 leaves, with a shoot forming at the base, and pinch out any other new growth. When you have harvested the fruit, prune out the fruited shoots and tie in the shoot at its base.

Bill Scott from Billericay, Essex. Has a shaded garden and wants to know which herbs he can most easily grow.

Most herbs require a sunny position to grow well but there are one or two more common types that will do alright in shade or semi-shade. Chervil and woodruff should thrive whilst mints, sorrel, lovage, angelica, sweet cicely, horseradish and bay will tolerate semi-shade.

A. Halpen in sunny Manchester. Has club root on an allotment site. How can we deal with this in an organic way please?

Unfortunately, there is no organic cure for club root which can survive in the soil for more years than we care to mention. The answer, therefore, is to only plant susceptible plants if they are strong and growing well. This can be achieved by raising the plants in pots. They will still be affected by the disease but will still be able to produce a decent crop because they will have had a good start in life.

Sylvia Ridley, Oakham, Rutland. Asks how do I grow bearded Iris in a shady, clay soiled garden? I love them but they always die.

The sad fact is that bearded Iris like to be grown in a well drained, fertile, neutral to acid soil in full sun, which sounds the complete opposite to the conditions you are able to give them. Our advice is to find a replacement that will fill your heart with as much joy, but that will grow in your garden.

Tracey West from Brighton. Noticed that you had lots of large leaves protecting the plants from frost at Barnsdale when she visited, what type of leaves were they?

The Gunnera leaves had been cut off the plants in the autumn and turned upside down over the crowns of the actual plant itself. This will protect the slightly frost sensitive crowns from any winter damage. Gunnera is a fantastic architectural plant for a boggy area and it even provides the material for its own protection!

Gerald Bebb keeps a small garden in Gloucester. He wants you to recommend a fragrant rose to grow on a trellis that is in shade until about 3pm every day.

There are several roses that fit the bill. 'Alberic Barbier' is creamy-white, 'Ena Harkness Climbing' is crimson, 'Felicite et Perpetue' is white, 'Mme Gregoire Straechelin' is clear pink, 'Mme Legras de St. Germain' is white, 'Mme Plantier is white', 'Mme Alfred Carriere' is blush pink, 'Maigold' is bronze-yellow, 'New Dawn' is blush pink, 'Mermaid' is yellow and 'Veilchenblau' is dark magenta. Enough to be getting on with we think.

Vic Arnold in Wimbledon. Says that insects play an important role in the garden, which specific plants and shrubs would you choose to attract the maximum variety?

To be honest a garden planted with a range of plants, shrubs and trees will attract and house many, many different insects but Buddleja, Helianthus, Limnanthes, Syringa, Eryngium, Lonicera, a wide range of herbs and of course many wildflowers will certainly do the job.

Mary Ross from Huddersfield. Planted a mulberry in the autumn and it is now May and it seems like it might just be starting into growth when all her other trees are in full leaf. Has she planted it in the wrong place?

The mulberry, or Morus nigra, is a funny tree, it comes into growth very late which is what sparked the saying 'once the mulberry has broken bud that is a sure sign the last frost has gone'. If it is planted in a sunny position and is now growing then all is well.

David Dunstan hails from Hull. He asks, why should we not put citrus fruit skins on the compost heap?

For our compost heap to work at its best it needs to be kept sweet. We are not suggesting that you buy it a box of chocolates and a bunch of flowers every now and then, but do keep it on the alkaline side of the pH scale. Citrus skins are acidic so too many will turn your heap sour. You can get away with a few from time to time and if you think you may have overdone it, balance the skins out with the addition of some lime.

Mrs. J. Radford lives in Brighton. She wants to know which palms can be grown in this country.

To a temperature of minus 15 degrees centigrade Trachycarpus fortunei will survive, so it should do just fine in a sunny, sheltered spot in your garden. Its pet hate is the wind.

Mr. M J Dyson from Suffolk. Would like to know if it has been scientifically proven that organically grown vegetables and fruit are better for you.

At Barnsdale we like to look at that question from the other perspective which is, "Are inorganic vegetables and fruit not as good for you as those that are organically grown?" and our answer to that would be yes. Logic, if nothing else, would tell you that if you ingest something neat or diluted that may kill or seriously harm you, it is likely to do you no good when consumed in much smaller quantities. There is not the research to prove this and there is unlikely to be in the near future, but we are much happier knowing what is on and in our home grown produce.

Mr. Morrisey lives in Streatham, London. He says that he has heard that you can store leeks to save having to chisel them out of frozen ground in winter. What is the method?

It is quite simple and will keep your leeks fresh and easy to harvest for quite some time. Just dig a trench about a spit's depth and put your leeks in it so that they are standing upright against the back wall of the trench and back fill it with the loose soil. Then firm down with your boot and leave until frosty weather. When required these can be easily removed as they are only covered with loose soil. It is best to rotate them regularly by using the stored ones and replacing with fresh when it is possible to dig them up.

Lesley Formby from Sandy, Bedfordshire. Asks why do Parsley 'Moss Curled' seeds always germinate erratically?

The seeds of parsley have a built in safety device which keeps them dormant until the best conditions prevail for their ultimate survival. It is possible to break this dormancy by treating the seed with a covering of boiling water prior to sowing and then follow the usual sowing technique. This will ensure a uniform and excellent germination rate, but please wait until the water has cooled before removing the seeds!

Charlaine Woods from Bedfordshire. Asks a pertinent question, if we get a hosepipe ban and I cannot use my sprinkler, how do I stop my grass from going brown and dry?

The answer to this is quite simple but not as easy as turning on the tap and allowing the sprinkler to do the work for you. Recycling of water is the answer. Washing up water, water saved in a water butt and even bath water can all be reused on the lawn and borders. We know of somebody who siphons their bath water out of the bathroom window, with a hosepipe and fills a water butt which is then used to water various parts of their garden in summer.

Terry Clarke lives near Worcester. Says that every year his Pyracantha has neat semicircles eaten away from around the edge. What is causing this and should he spray the plant?

This damage is caused by a leaf weevil which is harmless in every other way. We do not worry about it and quite like the look of the effect it causes! If you want to control them then a proprietary contact insecticide should do the job.

Bill Killick from Barnet. Has a bergamot that gets covered with mildew every year, how can he prevent this?

It sounds like you either have Monarda 'Cambrige Scarlet' or 'Squaw', both of which are prone to mildew. Although they prefer a well drained soil the mildew takes hold when they are too dry so mulching will help and so will watering during dry spells. If it becomes all too much for you but you still want a bergamot in your garden then look to the ones named after the horoscope birth signs, such as 'Aquarius' and 'Scorpio' as they are all resistant to mildew.

Ted Smith from Southend. Has found some strange, brightly coloured, tropical looking plants appearing his garden – any idea as to where they could have come from?

This is a question we are often asked at Barnsdale and the answer is quite simple. They are growing from seed dropped by birds either from their beaks or the other end and will be from the bought bird seed they have been feeding on in somebody's garden. These plants are not winter hardy so enjoy them while you can.

Mrs. Alice Watts lives near Pakefield. Her mum is pestering her for a cutting from her rubber plant. How can she keep mum quiet!

We have found that the simplest way is to air layer in the summer. This involves cutting into the current year's growth, to wound the plant, dust this cut with hormone rooting powder and then wrap some moist compost, held in place with polythene, tied top and bottom around it. In about six months time the new plant should be rooted and can be cut away from the parent and potted up.

Jane Biggs in Leicester. Has an air plant that looks a bit sad, can you advise her as to how she should care for it please?

Air plants have no roots so they pull their nutrients and water from the air, if the humidity is low they can dry out. Therefore they benefit from a light misting or from having a bowl of water close by. They need minimal nutrients but if you sort out the humidity problem and it still looks sad, a minimal feed will help.

Ashley Warren lives near Rotherham. Wants to know how you get your pumpkins so large. *It's a bit of a personal question, Ashley, but Nick is prepared to answer it.*

Use the right variety to start with, something like 'Atlantic Giant'. We sow our pumpkins in April directly into 8cm (3") pots and then once they have rooted into this size pot we put them into a 3 litre pot. There is no point sowing too early as they cannot be planted outside until the last of the frosts has passed and if sown too early they will suffer from being in the pot too long. Pumpkins require a lot of water so we water ours every day, unless we have had a real downpour. They then swell into monsters that will give us plenty of pumpkin soup and pies.

James Battford from Towcester. Has a new plot of land that he cannot get to work on for a while. He wants to know the best method of preventing weeds growing on the area.

It is a good idea to put down a weed suppressant membrane across the entire plot. When you do get the chance to get planting, all you have to do is cut a cross in the membrane and then plant through it. The four flaps of the cross can then be pushed back snugly around the plant and then mulch to cover the membrane. The membrane will allow the passage of air to and fro but stop weeds.

Terry Sotherby gardens near Salisbury. Has grown Osteospermum 'Yellow Symphony', a lovely plant, for a couple of years but each winter they have died, she would like to know what she is doing wrong.

This Osteospermum, as with all upright varieties, is not British winter hardy, so would need to be dug up and moved into a frost free place for the winter. Try putting the plants in a greenhouse, conservatory or porch. They can then be put outside during late May/early June, in full bloom, to flower right through until the frosts start.

Mr. N. Summers lives in Watford in Hertfordshire. He says that he hasn't got any worms in his soil and wants some!

The good news is that worms just seem to appear in a well cultivated soil. The bad news is that well cultivated bit. If you dig plenty of well rotted organic matter into your soil each year your worm population will increase rapidly.

Part Five – Pilgrim on Pests and Helpful Bugs

Barnsdale is an organic garden where Nick and Sue encourage wildlife in an effort to combine the natural life of plants, trees, shrubs and all living things. I was inspired to include this section in our book because David Thrower decided to photograph some of the wildlife at Barnsdale and got very dusty in the process! And because Johanna Pilgrim enjoys drawing bugs and beetles. The following is not an exhaustive list but it does include some of the more common 'goodies' and 'baddies' and how to accommodate them (or not).

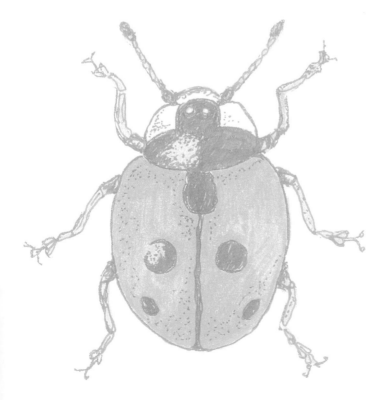

And First the Pests!

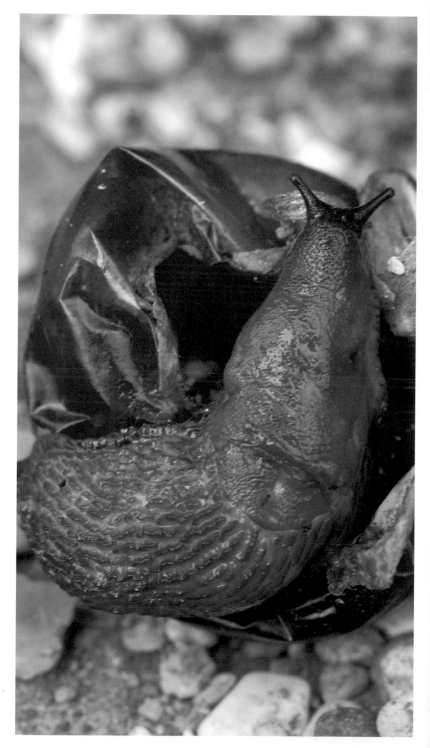

Aphids – Greenfly, Blackfly, Woolly Aphid, etc

In all their various forms, these pests are the bane of gardeners' lives inside and out, there is no escape! They are sap-sucking insects that feed from tender, young growths and can quickly colonise plants causing them great distress, distortion and in very severe cases even death. Sometimes they will feed on buds prior to growth and then the effects of the attack may not be noticed until long after the aphid has disappeared.

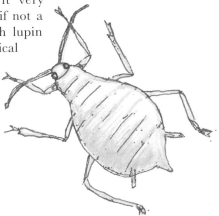

Each year Barnsdale has an attack of lupin aphid after their lupins

have flowered. The flowered stems become packed with the little blighters to a degree that it looks like the whole stem is alive and moving! A side effect of their presence is the black sooty mould that grows on the leaves directly below where they are feeding. This mould forms on the sticky excretions from the aphids and, although it does not directly harm the plant itself, it will prevent maximum photosynthesis and therefore weaken the plant. In small doses Nick and Sue love aphids because they are a vital source of food for much of the wildlife they like to encourage in their gardens. However, when an attack becomes greater than they are prepared to tolerate, it's time to bring in the heavy artillery and they don't get much heavier than the larvae of lacewings, hover-flies and ladybirds. Bats, birds, earwigs, spiders, ground beetles and wasps will also help to keep down the populations. The habits and benefits of all these predators are extolled in the next section. Nick always finds it very satisfying and very effective, if not a little messy, to simply squash lupin aphids using the very technical finger and thumb method, although this does somewhat contribute to the Hamilton Madness Syndrome Sue keeps telling him that he suffers from.

Cabbage Root Fly

You've probably seen them but not realised it. They resemble a horsefly but unlike the horsefly they are not bloodsuckers but egg layers. The larvae attack any plant in the brassica family so cabbage, brussel sprouts, radish, turnip and swede, etc. are all susceptible and in a severe attack it can damage root crops to the point at which they become inedible. The easiest and most effective method for stem-producing plants is to put a cabbage root fly mat around the stem of each individual plant at the planting stage. These can be bought at most garden centres but at Barnsdale they prefer to make their own from cheap carpet underlay. As the adults lay their eggs close to the stem it's important to have a tight fit, so cut out 10-12cm (4"-5") squares and cut into the middle on one side so that the mat can be slipped onto the stem snugly and then sit on the soil surface,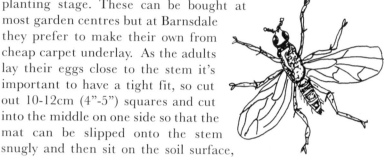
preventing the fly from laying its eggs close to the plant. For root brassicas this method is not feasible so Nick covers his with 'enviromesh' at sowing or planting stage and doesn't remove it until the crop is mature and therefore not so tasty to the larvae. There might be several egg laying cycles through the year and the pupae can even over winter in the soil, so crop rotation is as vitally important as the preventative method described above.

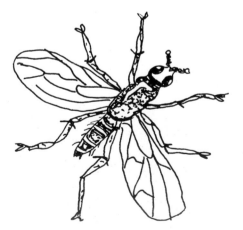

Cabbage White Butterfly

In the main, they encourage butterflies at Barnsdale and even like to see this one fluttering around the garden, but what they don't like is having to deal with cabbages and vegetables after a bad attack of cabbage white butterfly, prior to cooking. Nick eats anything and Sue doesn't mind the odd portion of holey cabbage but try feeding what resembles a green string vest to children or teenagers and you'll probably have as much joy as she does, so protection is vital. Nick covers all brassicas with netting immediately after planting and this proves to be very effective, but make sure the holes are not big enough for the butterfly to get through. If netting is not an option then regular evening checks to remove caterpillars and squash eggs is essential, as vigilance will save a lot of time later in the kitchen. There are two types of caterpillar to look out for, a hairy yellow and black one from the large white butterfly and a velvety-green one from the small white butterfly. Would you believe that wasps, of all things, are an excellent predator of the cabbage white butterfly caterpillars? There are non organic sprays which can be used if required but Nick tends to use Bacillus thuringiensis which is organic and is sprayed onto the brassicas at the first sighting of the butterflies. The caterpillars ingest it whilst eating your crop and the bacterium kills them from the inside. Although this is very effective and totally harmless to humans, as the bacterium is caterpillar specific, it is unfortunately becoming harder and harder to get and seems to be now only available to farmers in large 25kg bags, which would last the average gardener about 72 years!

Carrot Fly

There are few gardeners who ever actually see this little beast but its damage can be devastating to a nurtured crop of carrots, celery, parsnip or parsley. It's not the small shiny, black adult flies that cause the damage but the tiny, creamy-white larvae. The adults lay their first lot of eggs in the spring, usually in late May, next to their host plant. The larvae hatch and burrow into the roots and use them as their source of food before pupating into the adult flies and the cycle then starts again. There will usually be two, maybe three cycles a year, but it's normally the first one that does the most damage.

As the adults are attracted to the smell of the young roots, particularly after thinning, it's advisable to delay sowing until June and sow sparingly to avoid the need for thinning out later. It has been said that growing onions or garlic next to a crop will confuse the carrot fly although the effect only lasts until the onion or garlic starts to form a bulb. Carrot flies are not very strong flyers so they'll be more likely to attack in a still, sheltered garden than one that is more exposed. Nick also protects his carrots with either fleece or enviromesh. Both of these products, when fixed down, provide an impenetrable barrier to the pest, producing near perfect carrots, as well as having the added benefit of providing a better microclimate around the carrots, which encourages an earlier crop. Once the crop has gone past that young, succulent root stage the covering can be removed. Be warned! The larvae can over winter in the soil so do be sure to rotate your crop and thoroughly dig over the area to expose the larvae to the winter frosts which should kill them off.

Codling Moth

It's difficult to detect this pest until you bite into an apple or a pear and notice a hole made by it. In fact, you might notice a maggot in your mouth! The moth lays its eggs on the surface of the fruit and then they tunnel their way through to its centre. A pheromone trap will sort out two or three trees. Hang it in one of the trees and the pheromone will give off the scent of a female moth in search of a mate! The unwitting males fly into the trap looking for a good female only to be trapped on to the sticky pad. This lowers the amount of egg fertilization thus lowering the amount of fruit damage.

Earwigs

These little blighters can actually be of some benefit but it's up to you to decide as to whether the good outweighs the bad. If you want to get rid of earwigs then avoid growing susceptible plants against wooden fences etc. Earwigs crawl to the tips of plants just as they are about to bud and they'll eat the small flowers and can also attack the leaves of plants. Chrysanths are particularly vulnerable. You can trap earwigs in the tried and tested way by using upturned flower pots stuffed with hay or straw. Each morning shake out the pots to remove the earwigs.

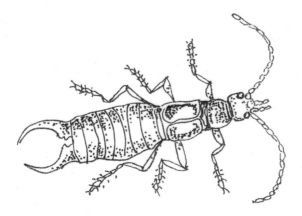

Flea Beetle

They are tiny and sometimes have yellow stripes on their outer wings. They will happily eat their way through the leaves of your seedlings and sometimes even fully grown vegetables. The most affected plants are radish, cauliflower, turnip, swede and cabbage. These beetles like the seedlings that lack water so the best defence is to keep your plants well watered in dry conditions. Nick says that his 'old man' really enjoyed his own particular method of doing away with these pests. They are called flea beetles because they jump sharply into the air when approached, so Geoff would coat a small piece of wood with grease (old engine oil is good) and pass the wood (grease side down) along the row of seedlings just above a cane which he ran along the tops of the leaves with the beetles then jumping up onto the greasy pad! You see, getting rid of garden pests organically can be fun! (You could also try just telling them to 'take a running jump'.)

Leaf Miner

The larvae of this pest eat out the tunnels that you see on some plants. The patches do eventually dry up and turn brown but apart from making the plant look unsightly, they do no real harm. There are different types of miner, some specific to certain plants such as apple, holly and beech. Pick off infected leaves and destroy them, away from the compost heap. If you fancy the 'Barnsdale Method' and want to go one step further like Nick, then squash the little devils.

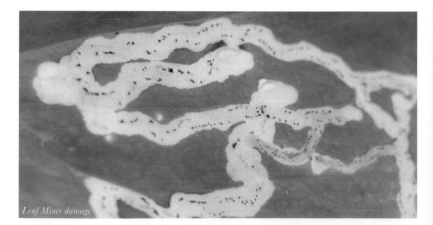

Leaf Miner damage

Leatherjackets

Geoff described them as being white, fat and very ugly and who am I to disagree. Leatherjackets are the larvae of the crane fly and are usually found just below the surface of the soil and they will eat almost anything. You may well notice them when you are digging over the ground, so keep your eyes open and remember Geoff's description and squash them! Ground beetles also enjoy a snack of leatherjackets so you could encourage them into your garden.

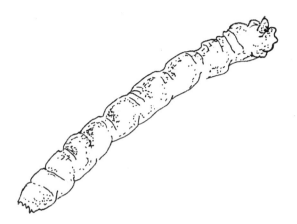

Mealy Bugs

Often they appear in large colonies on the undersides of leaves and they suck the sap from the plants. Mealy bugs can be controlled by encouraging hover-flies and ladybirds into the garden. Marigolds attract hover-flies as do nasturtiums. Companion planting is explained at the end of this section.

Mice

Although mice are not often a problem in the garden, when they do decide to give you a bad time they can do a lot of damage. In 2004, Nick and Sue planted a large number of bulbs and looked forward to a great show in 2005, but the mice took a fancy to the bulbs and the show never happened! Mice can also attack larger seeds such as peas and beans. The best way to defend your garden is with traps or to get yourself a cat. Naturally, owning a cat has some disadvantages but it is preferable to having next door's 'moggie' as a guest!

Moles

Yes, I know they are often portrayed as lovely, dozy little creatures and that is OK so long as they are not in your garden. They can do a great deal of damage to plant roots as they burrow around and of course, they enjoy eating the worms that you need for a healthy plot. Moles can often destroy a good lawn as well. You will find it difficult to keep moles completely away from your garden but smoke will drive them off temporarily and Geoff used holly leaves in their tunnels to make them feel uncomfortable. He didn't like killing these creatures but when all else fails traps do appear to be the best answer.

Rabbits

They look good and they taste good but they'll also eat almost anything from your garden and are difficult to eradicate. Keeping them out in the first place is the best solution and fencing is really the only way. Bury wire mesh (2.5cm – 1" is best) at least 15cm – 6" in the ground with 75cm – 30" above the ground.

Red Spider Mite

They are usually only a problem in a really dry year and they are difficult to spot. You know they are present when the leaves of plants take on a mottled, yellow appearance and they also spin visible webs. They like dry conditions so avoid any attack by spraying with water regularly.

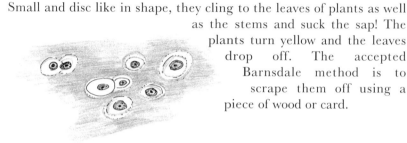

Scale Insects

Small and disc like in shape, they cling to the leaves of plants as well as the stems and suck the sap! The plants turn yellow and the leaves drop off. The accepted Barnsdale method is to scrape them off using a piece of wood or card.

Slugs and Snails

Both slugs and snails come in different sizes. The very large slugs feed on fungi and dead organic matter and so they're not likely to destroy your plants. The same cannot be said of the small brown or black ones! Some live underground and only come to the surface in mid summer – THIS IS THE TIME TO ATTACK! Some of the good old fashioned ways are still pretty effective, you can wander the garden at night when they are feeding, pick them up and pop them into a bucket to destroy later. It seems that Nick still uses this method (when he isn't watching Spurs play that is). You can also surround the plants with wood ash which will prevent them travelling, as it will absorb their slime. The big drawback is that any moisture such as rain will ruin your ash so it will need topping up. Try spreading a mulch of pine bark, or anything you can think of that the blighters will not enjoy crawling across.

Wasps

They will attack fruit as it ripens and can cause a lot of damage to trees and soft fruits as well. Often they'll go in after a bird has pecked at the fruit so try to protect the fruit from damage early on. To save your soft fruit from the birds (and therefore the wasps) use netting, plastic bags or, if you can, a fruit cage. You can also catch the wasps in a beer trap. Half fill a jar with some stale beer (not much of that left in Nick's garden shed) or maybe cider, in fact anything that is sweet. Cover the top with a piece of paper or polythene and make a small hole. It's an old trick but great organically in keeping them away from your fruit.

Weevils

There are many different species of weevil and they can cause a great deal of damage to all kinds of plants. The larvae are slimy and grow up to 6mm long, with yellowish-brown coloured heads. Vine weevils are currently our most serious type as they feed on plant roots and have the ability to devour enough to kill a plant in just a few days. Adult weevils spend the winter in the soil and in leaf litter, emerging in May or June when they lay their eggs on plants. There are two generations in one summer. If you want to remain organic as a gardener the best treatment is, yes you guessed it! Pick the adults off by hand and keep an eye on susceptible plants, especially potted ones, for the larvae, with the best control method being to squash the so and so's.

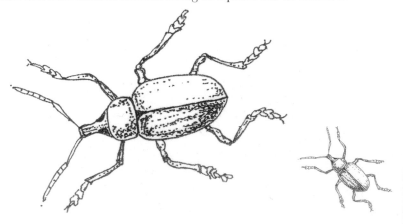

Whitefly

They are tiny and cause trouble both in the greenhouse and in the garden because they suck the sap from your plants. The good news is that they are attracted to anything yellow in colour so try a yellow card (Spurs supporters are used to seeing these, ask Nick) or a square of plastic and hang it up in the greenhouse coated with some sort of grease. The cabbage whitefly survives outdoors during the winter and they feed on any garden debris left around, so clear up after you!

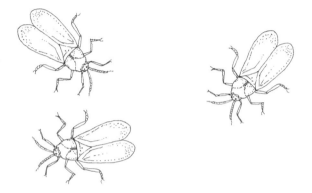

Wireworms

The larvae of the click beetle are shiny, thin worms with yellow skins. If you observe small holes in your potatoes or carrots that look like slug damage it could be these little chaps instead. They also enjoy plants with fleshy roots and this is the secret to controlling them. When you're cultivating newly turned soil grow a row of wheat between the crops at intervals. Do this during the first couple of years of cultivation. The wireworms are attracted to the wheat and you can dig it up and burn it. Old potatoes or carrots can be placed on a spiked stick and buried (remember to mark the spot) or you can use an old cabbage stalk in the same way, dig them up occasionally and remove the wireworms. My word, gardening can be fun can't it?

Woodlice and Millipedes

They can damage seedlings and young plants because they nibble away during the night when all good gardeners are in bed reading seed catalogues. Millipedes are black with short legs and are mainly found beneath the surface of the soil, feeding on roots. In both cases these pests breed under stones. The best way of getting these horrors out of your garden is to keep it clean, neat and tidy at all times and to regularly cultivate the soil. In this way you will expose them to the birds and hedgehogs.

Pilgrim on Helpful Wildlife

Companion Planting

Companion planting is based on the idea that plants have likes and dislikes when it comes to what they are planted close to. A great many of the ideas for companion planting come from folklore and it does seem to work. For instance, we know that the cabbage whitefly is attracted to its host by smell and that it can be fooled by planting French marigolds between cabbages. There is some scientific evidence for this as well. Nick and Sue aren't in any doubt when recommending the planting of marigolds near tomatoes or roses to reduce the threat of aphids, and the reason? Well, they attract hover-flies and the larvae of hover-flies are one of the best predators you can invite into your garden.

Bats

They feed on bugs, are wonderful to watch at twilight and have been much maligned in the past, but thankfully we now recognise that they are good to have around. An individual bat will consume about 3,500 insects per night. Obviously, they cannot differentiate between pests and beneficial insects, but will generally do gardeners more good than harm in that department.

Bumble Bees

Every garden should have them! In Britain the Bumble Bee is the largest species and they live in fairly small colonies, with only the fertilised queens surviving the winter. Being stung by a Bumble Bee is a pretty unlikely occurrence provided you don't give them hassle! The queen emerges from her winter rest around March when the weather warms up. The queen will lay about six eggs in a ball of wax and nectar and as the eggs hatch and grow she will add nectar and wax as required. You can encourage Bumble Bees into your garden by offering a good supply of pollen. Heathers, Primulas and Ribes are useful early flowerers, and do make sure that you offer a succession of flowers throughout the summer months. Supply a good nesting site by placing an old teapot in the ground with the spout exposed.

Honeybees

I once interviewed a bee-keeper for my radio programme and allowed myself to become covered in thousands of the wonderful creatures. Naturally, I wore protective clothing but it was a great experience and stimulated my interest in these 'gardener's friends'. Cave paintings have been found depicting man harvesting honey over eight thousand years ago. Honeybees, unlike other insects, remain active all year round and the honey they produce from plants sees them through the winter months. Male bees cannot sting and honeybees will swarm when they feel under attack, but under normal circumstances they are perfectly friendly creatures. Domestic hives can have as many as eight thousand bees working together in a structured order. A bee will be part of one of three castes: queens, drones or workers. If a colony of bees does enter your garden don't worry but do contact a member of your local bee-keepers' association, they will advise you as to what you should do. Remember, Honeybees are excellent pollinators.

Beetles

Ground beetles feed on eel-worms and leatherjackets and also enjoy the odd cutworm or two and other insect eggs. Encourage them into your garden by keeping the ground well covered as they like to hide under leaves during the day. You can also grow green manure plants between your crops in the vegetable garden. Nick swears by this method and recommends that you use mulches on your borders.

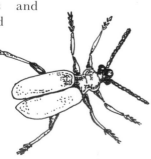

Birds

Some gardeners feel that all birds are pests in the garden, but they do more good than harm and anyway, a garden without birdsong isn't a proper garden is it? Grubs, caterpillars, slugs etc are all food for birds so make sure that you supply water for our feathered friends as well as a food table. Birds enjoy grass seed as well, so consider developing some of the more exotic grasses in your shrubbery, not forgetting to add a nesting box or two because these will encourage birds to return year after year. If you grow vegetables just remember that when raising a brood, a pair of blue tits will collect on average over 7,000 caterpillars.

Butterflies

Butterflies require a constant source of nectar and so you will need to provide as many nectar plants as possible. You will also need to ensure that you have plants to cover spring, summer and autumn. It's best to create your butterfly border in a sunny position and remember that if you want butterflies to breed in your garden, you will require some caterpillar food plants as well. A butterfly hedge is a good idea because it will offer shelter and provide protection for breeding as well as nectar, if you use the right plants. I have listed some below. For hedging use Catkins of sallow

(Pussy Willow), Holly and brambles but you can mix in privet and other attractive plants as well.

Elsewhere in the garden use Primrose, Red Campion, Clematis vitalba, Lonicera periclymenum and the following cultivated plants are useful as well: Buddleja, otherwise known as the butterfly bush is particularly good and try to use more than one variety if you can, Michaelmas daisy 'Barr's Pink', Sedum spectabile and varieties of Hebe.

Centipedes

These fast movers can suffer from ignorance when they are destroyed by manic gardeners who don't know that these bugs, which have longer legs than millipedes and only one pair per segment, eat small insects and slugs. They like ground cover during the day so that they can take a nap in preparation for their night-time attacks on your garden foes. They will even climb plants to find food.

Millipede   Centipede

Dragonflies

You don't necessarily need water to attract these wonderful creatures but it does help. They are fierce hunters and will eat almost any insects including other dragonflies! There are many species of dragonfly in this country; basically there are the 'darters' and the 'hawkers'. This describes the manner in which they hunt. The 'darters' have fatter and shorter bodies and they will perch somewhere quietly waiting for their chance to dart out on their prey, whereas 'hawkers' patrol an area looking for their prey.

Frogs and Toads

Just like our friend the mole, frogs and toads seem to bring out the best in people and that is good because every garden should have them. They love slugs, woodlice and other small insects. Although frogs only really need water to breed, to have a pond close by can be a great way to encourage them into your garden.

Hedgehogs

Spiky and crawling with bugs themselves, these little beasts are simply great for your organic garden because slugs, millipedes, wireworms and woodlice are their staple diet. If you're visited by a hedgehog do your best to encourage it to stay (they can be fickle). Cat food is one way to entice them to live in your garden I am told.

Hover-flies

"Thin wasps" is how Geoff described these creatures and very useful they are too. The adults lay their eggs in aphid colonies and the hatched young eat their way out. You can attract hover-flies by planting good old fashioned marigolds and nasturtiums as mentioned above under companion planting.

Lacewings

The larvae have a healthy appetite for aphids. The adult lacewing lays eggs on the underside of leaves and though they do not actually feed on flowers it's fairly easy to encourage them to your garden using various plants in an organised manner.

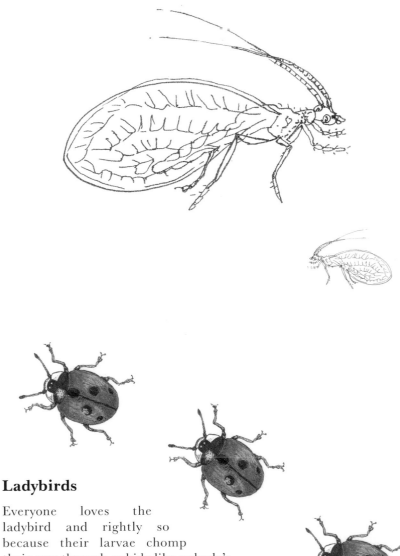

Ladybirds

Everyone loves the ladybird and rightly so because their larvae chomp their way through aphids like nobody's business and the adults are great to look at. It's not easy to actually encourage ladybirds into the garden with specific plants but if you choose carefully, they'll delight you and do you a favour along the way.

Index of Plants

Barnsdale Gardens are open every day of the year apart from two days over Christmas. For further details, please telephone 01572 813200 or check the website: www.barnsdalegardens.co.uk.

THE ARTISAN'S COTTAGE GARDEN

Built for the series "Geoff Hamilton's Cottage Gardens" on a very small budget. All the features are easily made by the average do-it-yourselfer and all the plants are easy to grow and to propagate.

Details of the materials used are available from the shop.